NEW
JEWISH COOKING

NEW
JEWISH COOKING

ELIZABETH WOLF COHEN

CHARTWELL
BOOKS, INC.

A QUINTET BOOK

Published by Chartwell Books
A Division of Book Sales, Inc.
110 Enterprise Avenue
Secaucus, New Jersey 07094

This edition produced for sale in the U.S.A.,
its territories and dependencies only.

ISBN 1-55521-926-8

This book was designed and produced by
Quintet Publishing Limited
6 Blundell Street
London N7 9BH

Creative Director: Richard Dewing
Senior Editor: Laura Sandelson
Designer: Pete Laws
Editor: Beverly Le Blanc
Photographer: Trevor Wood

Typeset in Great Britain by
Central Southern Typesetters, Eastbourne
Manufactured in Singapore by Eray Scan Pte Ltd
Printed in Hong Kong by
Leefung-Asco Printers Limited

TABLE OF CONTENTS

INTRODUCTION

Jewish cooking, defined by its international scope and kosher requirements, is one of the most interesting and varied cuisines in the world.

Many centuries ago, the Jews were banished from Palestine. They had no state. As the Jews migrated throughout the world, their cooking was borrowed from the local cuisine using native ingredients. While keeping their kosher requirements and observing their holiday customs, each group of Jews developed dishes suited to the country in which they had settled. Middle Eastern Jews, for example, used rice and aromatics with "exotic" vegetables in olive oil and Eastern European Jews salted herrings for use during the long winters and rendered goose or chicken fat for cooking hearty stews and potato kugels.

The main principle differentiating Jewish cooking from any other type of cookery is the principle of kashrut, the Jewish dietary laws commonly known as "kosher cooking". The rules of kashrut were derived from the Bible and Talmud and form a written code. Some of these rules have obvious reasons, others seem arbitrary, but they almost always take local traditions into account. Some say these early theological and symbolic rituals were devised to emphasize the Jews' separateness and oneness with God. In any case, these rules lay down a strict code of practice which is required for choosing and preparing foods, in accordance with holiday customs; this combination creates a distinct Jewish cuisine.

Broadly speaking, Jews fall into two groups, the Ashkenazic and Sephardic, although there are subgroups within each and, in some areas, the boundaries overlap. The Ashkenazic Jews came from Central and Eastern Europe, including Austria, Germany, Hungary, Poland and the former Soviet Union. However, as the Soviet Union was so large, some of the Jews near the Turkish and Iranian borders more closely resemble their Sephardic neighbors in their cooking traditions.

The Sephardic Jews came from Spain, Portugal and the Middle East. During the Spanish Inquisition at the end of the 15th century, many Jews were expelled from Spain and Portugal, some fleeing to Holland, while others returned to the Middle East. Interestingly, cooking slow-simmered stews for the Sabbath was considered by the Spanish as a sign of being Jewish and so a cause for expulsion.

Ashkenazic cooking tends to be subtle and delicate with many well-flavored, long-cooked dishes of beef and, sometimes, lamb with onions, paprika and sparingly used garlic. Parsley, dill and occasionally chives are the most frequently used herbs. Horseradish is the spicy accompaniment used for meat and fish dishes and always accompanies gefilte fish; pickles and gherkins are a favorite condiment. The combination of vinegar, lemon juice, or sour, and salt with sugar or honey creates a sweet-and-sour combination used in Germany, Hungary, Poland and the states of the former Soviet Union, in dishes such as sweet-and-sour cabbage and stuffed cabbage.

Much of the cooking of Central Europe was based on rendered goose or chicken fat, and smoked or salted fish, as these ingredients were inexpensive and widely available. Once potatoes were introduced from the New World, they became as popular as egg noodles, a specialty of Ashkenazic Jews and the base of many traditional dishes, such as kreplach and kugels. Barley, lentils and kasha are also popular ingredients.

Austrian, Hungarian and German Jews are renowned for their baking. During the great migration, at the end of the 19th century, of Europeans to the United States, German Jews set up bakeries in their adopted homeland. They sold strudels, cakes, yeast-cakes, challah, bagels and other breads and so these are now accepted as Jewish-American foods.

Fruit and vegetables are used widely in Ashkenazic cooking because they are pareve, or neutral, and can be eaten with meat or milk dishes.

In general, Sephardic cooking is characterized by the use of olive oil, lemon and garlic and of highly aromatic and, sometimes, very hot spices. Fresh herbs, such as dill and coriander, are used by Greek and Turkish Jews, but North African Jews prefer cumin and dried ginger. Almost all Sephardic Jews use cinnamon in both savory and sweet dishes.

Lamb is the favorite meat in most Sephardic kitchens, and saltwater fish is preferred to freshwater. Flat breads, such as pita, are eaten throughout the Middle East and some parts of the Mediterranean, as are olives, eggplant, zucchini, artichokes, tomatoes, peppers and beans. Although desserts are less important in Sephardic cooking than Ashkenazic, eggs and phyllo pastry with walnuts, almonds, cinnamon and rose- or orange-flower waters are more popular than dairy-based sweets.

The cooking of Morocco is particularly refined, influenced by the many years of French occupation. It combines the flavors and foods of the Sephardic tradition with the technical refinements of French cuisine. Spicy and aromatic, with saffron, lemon juice and salt-preserved lemons, garlic,

ABOVE A YEMENITE WITH TYPICAL *PEYOT* (SIDELOCKS) – THE ONLY NON-EUROPEAN JEWS TO WEAR THEM.

coriander, and the "sweet spices" – cinnamon, nutmeg, ginger, mace and allspice – all used generously. Yogurt is used throughout the Middle East, and tahini, a sesame paste, is important in the Eastern Mediterranean and Egypt.

The Jews of Italy, the majority of whom live in one of the oldest areas of Rome, generally cook in the Sephardic tradition, utilizing the many pasta dishes popular in Italian cooking and using the traditional Italian flavorings of rosemary, sage and basil.

In India, the Sephardic traditions are blended with the exotic flavors and spices of cumin, cinnamon, turmeric, cardamom, coriander seeds, garlic, ginger, chilies and fresh coriander. Indian Jews are divided into three groups, the Bene Israel Jews found mainly in Bombay, the Jews of Cochin on the Malibar Coast and the most recent immigrants, the Iraqi Jews. They arrived in the 19th century and settled in Bombay and Calcutta. The Iraqi Jews have combined their use of fresh herbs and greens with the spices and flavorings of India.

The establishment of Israel after World War II has had a tremendous influence on Jewish cooking. The Israelis developed great technological advances in agriculture, food production and the preparation of processed kosher foods. There is an exciting food revolution going on in Israel, led by a new generation of chefs who are working to combine many of the old traditions with the new technology and wide variety of foods now available.

Yemenite Jews from Arabia were among the settlers who flocked into the new Jewish state in 1949. Because they had been isolated for so long from the rest of the Jewish world they retained many of their customs and recipes in a pure form. Their exciting and spicy recipes which use cumin, turmeric, garlic, fresh coriander and a firey chili paste, called *Zhoug*, are being incorporated into the Israeli and Jewish repertoire.

With the continual changes and movements of peoples in the Middle East, especially in Israel, Jewish food continues to grow and evolve, while maintaining its traditions and rituals. These factors combine to produce one of the most exciting and satisfying cuisines in the world.

KASHRUT — DIETARY LAWS

Kashrut, the Jewish dietary laws for keeping kosher, or clean and proper, are long and sometimes complicated. Based on Divine Law, they find their roots in the Bible and Talmud, the teachings of Judaism. Keeping kosher is a way of life which involves the selection, preparation and combination of foods in accordance with traditional Jewish ritual and law. It certainly indicates the importance of cooking and food in the life of a Jew!

MEAT (FLEISHIG) AND POULTRY

In the Torah, the Jewish Bible, kosher animals are defined as quadrupeds which chew the cud and have cloven hooves: beef, veal, lamb, deer and goat are kosher; pork is not. Neither is horsemeat, camel, rabbit or hare. Poultry is kosher; birds of prey, freshly shot pheasant and other game birds, and scavengers are not. Local tradition is also important when determining what is kosher. Some Middle Eastern Jews will not eat geese because "they are of land and sea," yet geese were a staple part of the Eastern European Jews' diet.

For meat and poultry to be kosher, they must be slaughtered in the traditional way by a qualified *shohet*, or slaughterman. A special razor-sharp, smooth knife, twice as long the width of the animal's throat, severs at once the jugular vein, trachea, esophagus and two vagus nerves, causing as little pain and suffering to the animal as possible. The claws and the skin of the feet must also be removed.

As much of the blood as possible is drained away to conform with the Torah's prohibition against the consumption of blood. This is why as much blood as possible must be removed before cooking. This process is generally done by the butcher, but is also done at home to ensure all blood is removed. The meat or poultry is first soaked in cold water for 30 minutes in a receptacle especially for that purpose. It is then rinsed and evenly sprinkled with coarse salt, known as kosher salt, and placed on a perforated draining board for 1 hour. The salt is then shaken off and the meat or poultry rinsed 3 times and drained. Ground meat should be bought koshered or ground after koshering.

Liver and chicken livers require salting, then broiling on a rack or over an open fire to remove all blood and cook the flesh completely. Hearts must be cut open and all veins removed and blood drained before soaking and salting. Nowadays, most kosher meat bought in the U.S. will have been koshered before salting.

Certain parts of the animal are not kosher and cannot be eaten by Jews. Only the forequarters of the permitted quad-

> FOR RECIPES IN THIS BOOK, IT IS ASSUMED THAT MEAT AND POULTRY HAVE BEEN KOSHERED IN THE ACCEPTED MANNER. THEREFORE THESE INSTRUCTIONS DO NOT APPEAR IN EACH RECIPE. WHERE BUTTER OR MARGARINE ARE USED, VEGETABLE PAREVE MARGARINE SHOULD BE SUBSTITUTED FOR A KOSHER RECIPE. CHICKEN FAT CAN BE REPLACED WITH A VEGETABLE-BASED SUBSTITUTE. FOODS AND INGREDIENTS USED IN PASSOVER RECIPES SHOULD BE APPROVED KOSHER FOODS.

rupeds are acceptable. The hindquarter meat can be made kosher by "porging," that is removing the veins and sinews, but this process is so time-consuming and expensive it is rarely done.

FISH AND SHELLFISH

Not all fish are kosher; only fish which have scales and fins are kosher. Shellfish, crustaceans, eels and fish without true scales, such as catfish, monkfish, shark, European-turbot and sturgeon (therefore, unfortunately, caviar) are not kosher. No special koshering is required for fish; fish is pareve, or neutral.

MEAT AND MILK

"Thou shalt not seeth a kid in its mother's milk" (Deuteronomy 14:20) provides the basis for the prohibition of eating meat and milk or dairy products together. This was also a way of symbolically rejecting the pagan custom of animal sacrifice; it was also believed to aid digestion. Even now in certain Jewish communities, it is customary to wait up to 6 hours after eating meat before eating foods which contain milk. However, after a milk dish or meal, it is necessary to wait only 1 hour before eating meat.

These laws are observed by keeping separate utensils, cookware, plates, silverware, and even dishwashers! (Glassware can be used for both meat and milk, as it is not porous.) Milk and meat should be stored separately and away from each other in the refrigerator. Milk, or dairy meals, called *milchig*, are meals which contain milk or milk products, such as butter, some margarines, cheese or yogurt. Meat, *fleishig*, refers to meat or poultry dishes. (Milk substitutes such as soya milk can be used for custards, sauces and other foods.)

ABOVE DRIED FRUIT AND NUTS — CHARACTERISTICALLY SEPHARDIC INGREDIENTS.

PAREVE FOODS

Foods which are neither meat, poultry or milk-based are considered neutral, or pareve. All fruits and vegetables, as well as fish, eggs, vegetable oils and vegetable margarines may be eaten with a meat or milk dish. Eggs must be examined for blood spots; any spot indicates a fertilized egg and the egg must be discarded. It is always advisable to break an egg into a saucer to examine it before adding to any recipe.

CHEESE AND GELATIN

Natural rennet, which is used to curdle the milk in cheese-making, is produced from the stomach of a ruminating animal – most often a cow. Therefore most natural cheeses are not kosher. Many vegetarian cheeses, however, are made with rennet substitutes and can be eaten. Many new kosher cheeses are coming onto the market. The same is true for gelatin, which is made from animal bones. Kosher gelatin is made from kelp, a seaweed, and is an acceptable substitute. Many non-Jews and vegetarians seek out kosher milk products as they are vegetable-based.

ALCOHOL

Wine has been drunk by Jews since Biblical times and remains part of the Sabbath ritual, as well as other holidays. Wines and liqueurs containing wine, fermented grapes and/or brandy must be labeled "kosher." To be kosher, the grapes must be harvested and processed under authorized supervision. Nowadays, California, Israel, France and other wine-producing countries produce high-quality kosher wines. Spirits and grain alcohols are also allowed.

KOSHER FOR PASSOVER

During Passover, breads, foods made with yeast, such as beer, flour and other leavening agents are strictly forbidden. These foods are generally replaced with matzo meal or potatostarch. Passover customs vary according to local traditions. Sephardic Jews may eat rice, but Ashkenazic Jews may not. In all communities, however, the setting of the Passover Sedar table is special and the choice of foods for this ceremonial dinner have symbolic value. The foods vary from one community and country to another, but wherever Jews are, the rituals are always followed.

TRADITIONAL FOODS AND CONDIMENTS

ZHOUG

ABOUT ½ CUP

This is a firey condiment or relish made from chili paste which is used extensively in Yemenite cooking. It is extremely *hot* and a little goes a long way. Stir this into stews and vegetable dishes for a spicy flavour, or serve as a condiment with pita sandwiches, kabobs or Falafel (see page 23). It can be made with red or green chilies.

- 5 to 6 fresh chili peppers
- 3 to 4 garlic cloves, peeled
- ¾ teaspoon salt
- Freshly ground black pepper
- 1 teaspoon ground cumin
- ¼ teaspoon ground cardamom

☐ Wearing rubber gloves, core and seed chili peppers. (Seeds will make it even hotter.)

☐ Into a food processor fitted with metal blade, place chilies and garlic and process until very finely blended. Mixture should be like a paste. Add 1 to 2 tablespoons of water and remaining spices. Process to blend. Store in a tightly covered jar 1 week.

LEBNAH

ABOUT 3 CUPS

Lebnah is a delicious, soft cream cheese made from yogurt throughout the Middle East. I first tasted it made by an Iranian woman and have been addicted ever since. It has a smooth, creamy texture and slightly acidic taste, which goes well with sweet or savory foods. Often shaped into balls and preserved in olive oil, lebnah can be bought in Middle Eastern grocery stores, but is easy to make at home.

- 4 cups good-quality plain yogurt
- 1 teaspoon salt
- Olive oil (optional)
- Chopped fresh parsley (optional)

☐ Dampen a double thickness of cheesecloth or a clean, thin dish towel and use to line a strainer. Place lined strainer over a large bowl.

☐ Mix yogurt with salt and pour into lined strainer. Cover surface with extended ends of the cheesecloth or dish towel and leave in a cool place overnight, or until liquid or whey has stopped dripping.

☐ Unmold on to a shallow dish or bowl and serve as any fresh cheese. Alternatively, with your hands, shape cheese into walnut-size balls. Arrange in a shallow dish and drizzle with olive oil; sprinkle with chopped parsley. Serve with warm pita bread.

SEPHARDIC HAROSET

ABOUT 2 CUPS

Haroset is a blend of fruits and nuts served at the Passover sedar to symbolize the mortar and bricks used to build the Egyptian pyramids, and to sweeten the bitter herbs on the Sedar plate. The combinations are innumerable: Ashkenazic recipes usually include apples, almonds or walnuts, cinnamon and wine, while Sephardic versions include dates, walnuts, raisins, oranges, figs, coriander and many other exotic ingredients.

- ¾ cup blanched almonds
- ¾ cup walnut pieces
- 2 cups fresh dates, pits removed
- 1 cup raisins
- 1 pomegranate, cut in quarters, seeds removed and juice reserved
- 1 teaspoon ground cinnamon
- ½ teaspoon ground ginger
- ¼ teaspoon cayenne pepper
- ¼ teaspoon ground cloves
- ¼ teaspoon ground cardamom
- 1 to 2 tablespoons orange juice

☐ In a food processor fitted with metal blade, process nuts until coarsely chopped, or finer if you like. Turn into a medium bowl.

☐ Add dates and raisins to processor and, using pulse action, process until chopped, 10 to 15 seconds. Do not overprocess or dried fruit may turn pastey. Add to nuts. Add pomegranate seeds and juice to processor and process until finely chopped.

☐ Stir into nuts and fruit and add the spices. Taste and adjust spices. Moisten with orange juice. Chill before serving.

ABOVE YOU CAN FIND EVERYTHING YOU NEED FOR THE JEWISH TABLE INSIDE THIS TYPICAL NEW YORK CITY DELI.

ASHKENAZIC HAROSET

ABOUT 3 CUPS

- 2 cups walnut pieces or pecan halves
- 2 large dessert apples, quartered and cored but unpeeled
- 2 tablespoons sugar or light brown sugar

- 1 teaspoon ground cinnamon
- ¼ teaspoon ground allspice
- Grated zest and a little juice of 1 lemon
- 2 to 3 tablespoons kosher sweet wine

☐ In a food processor fitted with metal blade, process nuts until coarsely chopped, or finer if you like. Turn into a medium bowl.

☐ Add apple quarters to processor and, using pulse action, process until chopped, 10 to 15 seconds. Do not overprocess or mixture will be too soggy.

☐ Add apple to bowl and stir in remaining ingredients until mixed. Taste and add more sugar or lemon juice if you like. Chill before serving.

BEET EINGEMACTS

ABOUT 2 PINTS

This preserve is served at Passover, as are many other beet dishes in the Ashkenazic repertoire. Although not often seen today, this is easy to make and delicious eaten on matzos with tea as the Ukranian, Lithuanian and Russian Jews used to do. For long term storage, follow manufacturers' directions on canning jars; otherwise make a small enough quantity to consume over Passover and store in the refrigerator. A similar preserve can be made with black radishes.

- 1 cup sugar
- 1 cup honey
- 1 tablespoon ground ginger
- 3 pounds beets, cooked, peeled and cut into thin strips or grated
- 2 lemons, cut in half lengthwise, seeds removed and thinly sliced
- ¾ cup blanched almonds, chopped

☐ In a large nonmetalic saucepot or kettle, over medium-high heat, bring sugar, honey, ginger and ½ cup water to a boil. Simmer until sugar is dissolved and liquid syrupy, 5 to 7 minutes.

☐ Add beet strips and lemon slices and stir to blend. Bring to a boil, then reduce heat and cook until mixture is very thick and forms a mass, shaking pan occasionally so mixture does not stick, 30 to 40 minutes. Stir in almonds.

☐ Prepare canning jars according to manufacturers' directions and spoon mixture carefully into jars. Alternatively, rinse jam jars in water and heat in 350°F oven for 5 to 7 minutes. Fill jars with mixture. Cool them and cover with lids. Use within 2 to 3 weeks.

SCHMALTZ AND GREBENES

ABOUT ¾ CUP

Schmaltz and grebenes have fallen from favor as medical science draws the link between animal fats and coronary heart disease. In Central and Eastern European cooking, schmaltz was rendered from chicken, goose or duck fat and used to cook in as well as to season whole dishes. Old-fashioned chopped chicken liver depended on it. Nowadays, however, we use butter, margarine or oil, but occasionally potatoes fried in schmaltz are for something special. Grebenes are the small pieces of skin or crackling which are also added to chopped liver or potato dishes or eaten on their own like potato chips.

- Chicken skin
- ½ pound chicken, goose or duck fat from cavity and outside the
- bird, cut into small pieces
- ½ onion, chopped (optional)

☐ In a medium saucepan, over low heat, combine chicken skin and fat with ¼ cup water. Cook until the fat has melted and water is evaporated. The skin and onion should be crisp and brown. Strain fat (schmaltz) into a small bowl. Drain skin (grebenes) and onion bits on paper towels. Store both covered in refrigerator and use for frying or roasting.

EGGS IN SALT WATER

6 SERVINGS

This dish was traditionally served only on the Passover Seder table, to represent the sacrifice to the temple; a symbol of mourning for the death of the Temple, and as a symbol of birth or life. This is an old tradition still used today.

- 3 teaspoons salt
- 6 eggs, hard-boiled and shelled

☐ In a large bowl or soup terrine, combine salt with 4 to 5 cups water. Stir until dissolved. About 30 minutes before serving add whole eggs; refrigerate until ready to serve. Ladle each egg with a little salt water (½ cup) in to 6 small bowls and serve to each person.

TAHINI SAUCE

Tahini paste is made from sesame seeds. It is most often used to make a sauce or dip served on the *meze* tables of Greece, Cyprus, Israel and the Middle East. Sold in cans or jars, it is easy to use. A friend of mine, who was born in Cyprus, always serves it as a sauce when we barbecue lamb or chicken. This sauce has a distinct taste and texture which goes well with grilled foods and salads.

- 1 garlic clove, peeled and crushed
- ½ cup tahini paste
- ¼ cup lemon juice
- ¼ teaspoon salt
- Chopped fresh parsley or coriander for garnish

☐ Rub a small serving bowl with the garlic, then leave garlic in bowl. Add tahini paste and, using a fork, blend in ¼ cup water, lemon juice and salt. Wipe edges of bowl and sprinkle with chopped parsley or coriander.

HORSERADISH-BEET SAUCE

ABOUT 3 CUPS

Horseradish, *chrein* in Russian, is considered one of the bitter herbs presented for the Passover table. This sauce is popular with gefilte fish, corned beef and other meats. Fresh horseradish can be found in Chinese supermarkets, and it is like chilis or onions – it can burn your eyes and skin, so wear rubber gloves when preparing it and use a food processor for grating, if possible.

- 1 medium fresh horseradish root
- 3 to 4 beets, cooked, peeled and cut to fit food processor tube
- 1 tablespoon light brown sugar or honey
- Freshly ground black pepper
- ¾ to 1 cup distilled white or cider vinegar

☐ Wearing rubber gloves, use a swivel-vegetable peeler, peel horseradish root. Trim ends. In a food processor fitted with grating disc, grate horseradish.

☐ Without removing processor cover, grate cooked beets on to horseradish.

☐ Remove cover and scrape into a medium bowl, mixing well with brown sugar or honey, pepper to taste and vinegar. If mixture is too dry, add a little more vinegar. Store refrigerated in a covered jar.

COOK'S TIP

HORSERADISH VARIES IN PUNGENCY DEPENDING ON THE VARIETY AND ITS AGE, SO TASTE A TINY AMOUNT OF MIXTURE AND ADJUST THE SEASONING ACCORDINGLY.

Appetizers and Soups

Piroshki

Chopped Herring

Herrings in Sour Cream

Chopped Liver

Calves' Foot Jelly

Baba Ganoush

Falafel

Hummus

Artichokes, Jewish Style

Cheese Knishes

Peruvian Pickled Fish

Beet Borsht

Sweet-and-Sour Cabbage Soup

Mushroom and Barley Soup

Lentil Soup

Classic Chicken Soup with Matzo Balls

Italian Bean and Pasta Soup

Shchav

PIROSHKI

ABOUT 38 PIECES

Piroshki are tiny pastries, originally from Russia, usually eaten with a clear meat or chicken broth, but also delicious on their own. With the tremendous exodus of Russian Jews to America and Israel in recent years, these are becoming increasingly popular; they make a delightful canapé or hors-d'oeuvre. Traditionally made with a yeast-based dough, a good flaky pastry or commercial puff pastry can be used. The filling can vary from meat to fish, to mushrooms, to cheese and spinach, or any combination you like.

- 1 envelope active-dry yeast
- 1 tablespoon sugar
- ¼ cup lukewarm water
- 3 to 3½ cups all-purpose flour
- 2 teaspoons salt
- 1 cup lukewarm milk
- ½ cup unsalted butter (1 stick), melted and cooled
- 2 large eggs, lightly beaten
- Vegetable oil for greasing bowl
- 1 egg, beaten with a pinch of salt and a pinch of sugar, for glaze

MEAT FILLING

- 1 tablespoon vegetable oil
- 1 medium onion, finely chopped
- ½ pound ground beef or veal
- 1 teaspoon salt
- Freshly ground black pepper
- ¼ teaspoon dried thyme
- ¼ teaspoon grated nutmeg
- 1 egg, lightly beaten

☐ Prepare dough. In a small bowl, combine yeast with sugar and lukewarm water. Leave to stand until mixture begins to foam, 10 to 15 minutes.

☐ In a large bowl, mix 3 cups of the flour and salt and make a well in center. Add foamy yeast mixture, lukewarm milk, melted and cooled butter and beaten eggs. Stir mixture until a soft dough begins to form.

☐ Turn out dough on to lightly floured work surface and knead dough gently, adding a little flour if necessary to keep dough from sticking. Dough will become smooth and slightly elastic after 10 to 15 minutes kneading.

☐ Form dough into ball and place in an oiled bowl. Cover with a clean dish towel and leave in a warm place until dough doubles in bulk, 1 to 1½ hours. Punch down dough, cover and refrigerate overnight. (If dough is needed quickly, cover and leave to rise again in a warm place for about another hour.)

☐ Prepare filling. In a medium skillet, over medium heat, heat oil. Add chopped onion and cook until onion is soft and begins to color, about 5 minutes. Add ground beef or veal and cook, stirring occasionally, until meat has lost its pink color and any liquid has evaporated, 5 to 7 minutes. Season with

salt, pepper, thyme, and nutmeg and remove from heat to cool slightly. Mix in the beaten egg, turn into a medium bowl and refrigerate, covered, until ready to use. (Filling can be prepared several hours ahead or overnight.)

☐ Lightly grease 2 large cookie sheets (you will need to work in batches). Cut dough into 3 or 4 pieces, work on one piece at a time and keep remaining dough refrigerated.

☐ On a lightly floured surface, roll out dough about ⅛ inch thick. Using a 3-inch round cutter, cut out as many circles as possible. Brush edge of each circle with a little egg glaze. Place 1 rounded teaspoon of filling on each circle and fold to form a half-moon shape; carefully press edges together. Repeat by rerolling any scraps of dough.

☐ Place on cookie sheet, cover with a clean dish towel and leave in a warm place to rise, 20 minutes. Preheat oven to 400°F.

☐ Brush top of each half-moon with a little egg glaze and bake until golden brown and puffed, 15 to 20 minutes. Serve warm with a little sour cream or yogurt.

> **COOK'S TIP**
>
> PIROSHKI CAN BE MADE
> AHEAD AND REFRIGERATED.
> REHEAT IN A 350°F OVEN
> 5 TO 7 MINUTES BEFORE
> SERVING.

ABOVE DEVOUT JEWS WEARING *TEFILLIN* (BOXES BOUND WITH LEATHER WHICH CONTAIN PASSAGES FROM THE SCRIPTURES) IN A MOSCOW SYNAGOGUE.

CHOPPED HERRING

4 TO 6 SERVINGS

In the poor Eastern European communities, herring was traditionally eaten after breaking the fast of Yom Kippur to restore salt in the body. Chopped herring is a very popular appetizer among British and South African Jews and is often found on the Friday night table. My South African editor swears by her mother's Chopped Herring. This is her recipe.

- 12 tea biscuits
- 4 Granny Smith apples, quartered and cored but not peeled
- 4 eggs, hard-boiled and quartered
- 4 salted herrings, filleted, skinned and soaked overnight
- ¼ cup distilled white or cider vinegar
- Freshly ground black pepper
- ¼ teaspoon ground cinnamon
- 1 to 2 teaspoons sugar
- Fresh parsley for garnish

> **COOK'S TIP**
>
> MATZOS CAN BE SUBSTITUTED FOR THE TEA BISCUITS IF YOU WISH TO SERVE THE DISH DURING PASSOVER.

☐ In a food processor fitted with metal blade, process tea biscuits until fine crumbs form. Pour into a large bowl. Add apple quarters and, using the pulse action, process until chopped, but not too fine or they will be too mushy. Add to bowl.

☐ Add egg quarters to processor and, using the pulse action, process 3 to 5 times until chopped. Do not overprocess or they will form a paste. Add eggs to bowl. Add herring to processor and process until chopped. Do not overprocess or they will form a paste. Add to bowl and stir.

☐ Stir in the vinegar, pepper to taste, cinnamon and sugar. You may need to taste to adjust the balance of vinegar and sugar. Spread the mixture on a flat serving dish, cover with plastic wrap and refrigerate until ready to serve. Garnish with sprigs of parsley.

HERRINGS IN SOUR CREAM

6 TO 8 SERVINGS

Herrings became a staple of the Jewish diet in Poland, Hungary, Czechoslovakia, and other Eastern European countries because they were economical. Herrings of all kinds are available today in Jewish delis. If using salt herrings, soak them in cold water for at least four hours.

- 1 16-ounce jar pickled herrings or herrings in wine sauce, drained
- 1 red onion, thinly sliced
- 4 Granny Smith apples, halved and cored but not peeled
- ½ tablespoon lemon juice or cider vinegar
- ½ teaspoon ground cinnamon
- 2 teaspoons sugar
- 1 cup sour cream or plain yogurt
- Freshly ground black pepper
- Radicchio and fresh dill sprigs for garnish
- Black bread for serving

☐ Pat herrings dry with paper towels. Discard onions and liquid from the jar. Lay each herring flat on cutting board and holding sharp knife at an angle, cut each into 5 to 6 diagonal slices. Remove to mixing bowl and add thinly sliced red onion.

☐ Lay each apple half cut-side down on cutting board and cut into thin slices. Add to herrings and onions.

☐ In a small bowl, combine lemon juice or vinegar, cinnamon, sugar and sour cream or yogurt. Season with black pepper.

☐ Pour dressing over herrings, onions and apples. Toss to blend well, cover with plastic wrap and refrigerate 2 hours or overnight.

☐ To serve, arrange a leaf or two of radicchio on individual serving plates, spoon on equal amounts of herring mixture and garnish with sprigs of fresh dill. Serve with black bread.

CHOPPED LIVER

6 TO 8 SERVINGS

This is probably the most well-known and best-loved Jewish dish. No one really knows its origins, but when it comes to chopped liver, everybody's an expert. Traditionally, chicken fat is used to cook the onions and bind the mixture, as well as provide a smooth texture. This version replaces the fat with vegetable oil which is less rich and lower in saturated fat. Use a kosher margarine if you prefer. Serve with rye bread, challah or matzo. For an elegant presentation, pipe on to small toasts or crackers.

- 1 pound chicken livers
- Salt
- Freshly ground black pepper
- 2 tablespoons vegetable oil
- 2 medium onions, chopped
- 4 large eggs, hard-boiled and chopped
- Chicken stock (optional)
- Shredded lettuce and cherry tomatoes for garnish

☐ Preheat broiler. Arrange livers on foil-lined broiler pan and sprinkle with salt. Broil until lightly brown, 3 to 4 minutes. Turn livers over, sprinkle with salt and broil until just cooked through, 3 to 4 minutes longer; livers should no longer be pink. Remove livers to cooling rack to drain and cool slightly.

☐ In a large skillet, over medium heat, heat oil. Add chopped onions and cook until soft and golden, 10 to 12 minutes, stirring occasionally.

☐ In a food processor fitted with metal blade, chop livers coarsely using the pulse action. Add onions and, using the pulse action, chop until livers and onions are just blended. Add chopped eggs, salt and pepper to taste and, using the pulse action, chop again until just blended. If mixture is dry, add a little more oil or a spoonful of chicken stock.

☐ Spoon mixture into a serving bowl, cover and refrigerate 2 hours or until ready to serve. Garnish with shredded lettuce and cherry tomatoes.

CALVES' FOOT JELLY

8 SERVINGS

Love it or hate it, this traditional dish is still very popular with Eastern European Jews. Well made, it resembles some of the more modern, low-fat cooking we prefer today. Mold the mixture in a loaf pan or terrine and serve slices garnished with fresh herbs for a contemporary look. Be sure to have your butcher cut the feet into pieces for easier handling.

- 4 calves' feet, cleaned, halved and cut into pieces
- 1 pound shin of veal, or 1 pound chicken legs
- 1 large onion, sliced
- 1 carrot
- 1 celery stalk
- 4 bay leaves
- 6 to 8 garlic cloves, peeled and slightly crushed
- 1½ teaspoons salt
- 1 tablespoon black peppercorns
- 2 tablespoons lemon juice or cider vinegar
- 3 to 4 large eggs, hard-boiled and sliced
- Lemon and fresh parsley sprigs for garnish

☐ Place cut-up calves' feet into a very large stockpot and cover with cold water. Over high heat, bring to a boil, then simmer gently for 5 minutes. Drain into a large colander and rinse feet well with cold water.

☐ Place feet in cleaned stockpot and cover again with cold water. Add all remaining ingredients, except lemon juice or vinegar, hard-boiled eggs and garnish. Over high heat, bring to a boil, then simmer for 5 minutes. Using a wet cooking spoon, skim off any froth that comes to the surface.

☐ Partially cover stockpot and simmer gently over low heat for 3 to 4 hours, skimming occasionally. The meat should be very tender and falling off bones.

☐ With a slotted spoon, carefully lift out calves' feet and any meat and remove to a cutting board. Strain liquid into a large heatproof bowl. Wash the pot and return liquid to cleaned pot with lemon juice.

☐ Remove gristle and meat from feet and cut into small pieces. Add meat to liquid.

☐ Ladle half liquid with meat into a terrine or deep dish and refrigerate until the liquid begins to set. Arrange hard-boiled egg slices on surface, pushing them in gently. Carefully spoon over remaining liquid and meat. Refrigerate overnight until firm and set.

☐ To serve, cut jelly from terrine or dish (or turn out on to serving platter.) Garnish with lemon and parsley.

ABOVE THE "BLUE DANUBE" FROM A VANTAGE POINT IN BUDAPEST.

BABA GANOUSH

8 TO 10 SERVINGS

There are many versions of this eggplant and tahini dip which is popular all over the Middle East. When I lived in a small studio in Paris, I was shocked to learn my Israeli neighbor "grilled" the eggplants directly on the electric hot plate in her even smaller studio.

Ideally, the eggplants should be grilled over a barbecue for 30 to 40 minutes until completely tender, the skins blackened and collapsed; this is what gives the dip its slightly smoky flavor.

- 2 medium eggplants, about 1½ pounds total weight
- ¼ cup lemon juice
- ¼ cup tahini (sesame paste)
- 3 to 4 garlic cloves, peeled and crushed
- Salt
- Freshly ground black pepper
- Olive oil
- Chopped fresh parsley and ripe olives for garnish
- Pita bread, warmed, for serving

☐ Preheat oven to 450°F. Pierce eggplants all over with a fork or sharp knife. Arrange on a cookie sheet and bake until completely tender and collapsed, 30 to 40 minutes. Cool slightly.

☐ Cut each eggplant in half lengthwise and scoop out flesh; place flesh in a food processor fitted with metal blade. Process eggplant until smooth.

☐ Add lemon juice, tahini, garlic and salt and pepper to taste and process until well blended. With the machine running, slowly add 2 to 3 tablespoons olive oil until the mixture is well blended and creamy. Adjust seasoning; spoon into a bowl, cover with plastic wrap, and chill for 2 hours or overnight.

☐ To serve, spoon into a shallow dish or individual plates and with the back of a spoon make a hollow in the center. Spoon in a little olive oil, sprinkle with chopped parsley and garnish with ripe olives. Serve with warm pita bread.

FALAFEL

ABOUT 30 PIECES

These spicy, fried garbanzo bean (chick-pea) balls could be called the Israeli national dish, although they are also eaten all over the Middle East. They can be eaten on their own, as part of a *meze* or in a pita bread with lettuce, tomato and cucumber. Zhoug and Tahini (see pages 11 and 15) are a must.

- 1 cup dried garbanzo beans (chick-peas), soaked at least 12 hours
- 1 slice day-old white bread, crusts removed
- 1 medium onion, quartered
- 4 to 5 garlic cloves, or to taste
- 2 tablespoons chopped fresh coriander or parsley
- 1 tablespoon ground coriander
- 1 tablespoon ground cumin
- 2 teaspoons salt
- Freshly ground black pepper
- ¼ cup bulgur, rinsed and drained, or 3 tablespoons all-purpose flour
- 1 teaspoon baking powder
- Vegetable oil for frying
- Pita bread for serving
- Israeli Salad (see page 89), hot pickles, zhoug, and tahini for serving

☐ Drain and rinse the garbanzo beans. Sprinkle bread with 1 tablespoon water and leave to soak in, then squeeze dry.

☐ In a food processor fitted with metal blade, process beans and bread to a semi-fine paste; you may need to work in batches. Turn mixture into a large bowl.

☐ Into processor, place onion quarters and, using pulse action, process until finely chopped. Add to bean purée and scrape processor well. Add garlic cloves to processor and process until finely chopped. Add coriander or parsley to garlic and continue to process until finely chopped. Add mixture to the beans and onions and mix well.

☐ Add ground coriander, cumin, salt and black pepper to taste. Stir in bulgur or flour and baking powder. Using clean hands, mix mixture very well.

☐ Using wet hands, shape about 1 tablespoon of mixture into a ball about the size of a walnut, rounding it between the palms of your hands; set balls on to a cookie sheet. Continue shaping until all mixture has been used. (Falafel can be prepared to this point several hours ahead.)

☐ In a deep-fat fryer or deep skillet, heat oil to 350°F. Add about one-quarter of the balls, sliding them carefully into the oil. Fry until a rich golden brown, 2 to 3 minutes. Remove with slotted spoon to paper towels to drain. Repeat with remaining balls, one-quarter at a time.

☐ Serve warm in pitas with Israeli Salad or with pickled peppers, zhoug and tahini.

HUMMUS

8 TO 10 SERVINGS

This creamy, golden purée of garbanzo beans (chick-peas) is a specialty of Middle Eastern Jews and non-Jews alike. It is popular as an appetizer or one of many dishes in a *meze* of Middle Eastern food. It is worth making a large batch as it keeps well in the refrigerator and is ideal to serve when unexpected guests arrive.

- 2½ cups dried garbanzo beans (chick-peas), or 4 15½- to 19-ounce cans, well rinsed
- Salt and cayenne pepper
- 4 to 6 garlic cloves, peeled and crushed
- ½ cup lemon juice
- ½ cup tahini (sesame paste)
- Olive oil, and chopped fresh parsley for garnish (optional)

☐ Rinse dried garbanzo beans very well, discarding any broken or discolored beans. Place beans in a large bowl and cover generously with cold water; soak 12 hours or overnight.

☐ Transfer beans and their soaking water to a large stockpot and, over medium heat, bring to a boil. Reduce heat and leave beans to simmer 1½ to 2 hours, until very tender.

☐ Add 1 teaspoon salt and continue simmering for 30 minutes. Drain well, reserving 1 tablespoon of beans and a little cooking liquid.

☐ Press cooked or canned beans through a food mill or strainer, adding reserved cooking liquid, to separate the beans from skins. (For a smooth hummus, skins must be separated from beans.) Discard skins.

☐ In a food processor fitted with metal blade, process crushed garlic with a pinch of salt. Add puréed beans and process until smooth. Add the lemon juice, tahini and a pinch of cayenne pepper and purée until finely blended. Hummus should be thick and smooth; add a little more cooking liquid if purée is too thick and adjust the seasoning. Transfer to a bowl and store in the refrigerator, covered, up to 5 days.

☐ To serve, spread hummus in a shallow dish or individual bowls and with the back of a spoon make a hollow in the center. Chop the reserved garbanzo beans coarsely and sprinkle over. If wished, pour a little olive oil in the center of the well, garnish with the chopped beans, parsley and a sprinkling of cayenne pepper.

ARTICHOKES, JEWISH STYLE

6 SERVINGS

This ancient specialty was introduced to Rome by Jews in the Middle Ages. It should be made with baby artichokes whose chokes have not yet developed now found in Italian groceries and fresh vegetable markets. Larger globe artichokes can be used, but the outer leaves and choke should be removed and the stems carefully trimmed.

- Juice of 2 to 3 lemons
- 12 small, young artichokes
- ½ cup olive oil
- 1 cup chopped fresh parsley (preferably Italian or flat leaf)
- ½ cup torn fresh basil leaves
- 1 teaspoon salt
- Freshly ground black pepper
- 8 to 10 garlic cloves, peeled and finely chopped
- Matzo meal
- Olive oil for frying
- Fresh parsley sprigs or basil leaves for garnish

☐ Place lemon juice in a large bowl and add enough water to fill bowl halfway.

☐ Discard any tough or damaged outer leaves from the artichokes. With a sharp knife, trim tops off artichokes and

peel stems if necessary; cut stems to 2 to 3 inches. As you prepare each artichoke, place it in bowl of water to prevent discoloration. Add more water if necessary.

☐ In a small bowl, combine olive oil, parsley, basil, salt, pepper to taste and garlic. Place ¾ cup of matzo meal in a pie plate; set aside.

☐ Drain artichokes well and pat dry with paper towels. Holding each artichoke by its stem, bang each top against a work surface to spread open leaves. Holding each by its stem, spoon a little oil and herb mixture between leaves, then roll each artichoke in the matzo meal.

☐ Cover bottom of a large Dutch oven or heavy skillet with about ⅛-inch olive oil; heat over medium heat. Place artichokes in pan and cook, covered, over medium-low heat, until tender and golden, 25 to 30 minutes, turning once or twice. Serve at room temperature with any cooking juices spooned over or drizzle with additional olive oil. Garnish with fresh parsley sprigs or basil leaves.

ABOVE HUMMUS.

CHEESE KNISHES

ABOUT 2 DOZEN PIECES

☐ Into a large bowl, sift flour, baking powder, salt and sugar. Transfer to a food processor fitted with metal blade. Add butter and process until mixture resembles fine crumbs. Remove cover and spoon the sour cream evenly over flour-butter mixture. Using pulse action, process until mixture begins to hold together. Do not allow dough to form into a ball or pastry will be tough. If dough appears too dry, add a little cold water, 1 tablespoon at a time.

☐ Turn out dough on to lightly floured work surface and knead lightly. Form dough into a ball and flatten; wrap well and refrigerate 2 hours or overnight. Leave dough to soften 15 minutes at room temperature before rolling out.

☐ In a large bowl, combine all filling ingredients until well blended.

☐ Lightly grease 2 large cookie sheets. Cut dough in half and work with one half at a time. Roll out dough to an 8- × 12-inch rectangle about ⅛ inch thick. Cut dough into 4-inch squares. Place cheese filling in center of each dough square.

☐ Brush edges of each dough square with a little egg glaze and fold lower-left corner up to upper-right corner to form a triangle. Using a fork press edges together to seal well. Place on cookie sheet. Continue with remaining dough and filling. You will need to bake in batches.

☐ Preheat oven to 400°F. Brush each triangle with a little egg glaze and score top of pastry to let steam escape. Bake until a rich golden brown, 17 to 20 minutes. Cool 15 minutes before serving.

Knishes, tiny filled pastries, are multipurpose, traditional Ashkenazic fare. Sometimes served with soup or on their own as an appetizer they are traditionally eaten at Shavuot with a moist cheese filling. Other fillings include potato, chicken and kasha (buckwheat groats). Many different kinds of pastry can be used but this sour cream pastry made in the food processor makes the whole job quick and easy.

PASTRY
- 2 cups all-purpose flour
- 1 teaspoon baking powder
- ½ teaspoon salt
- 1 teaspoon confectioners' sugar
- ½ cup (1 stick) unsalted butter or hard margarine, cut into small pieces
- ⅓ cup sour cream
- 1 egg, beaten, to glaze

CHEESE FILLING
- 1 8-ounce container cottage cheese
- 2 tablespoons sour cream
- 2 tablespoons fine matzo meal
- 1 tablespoon sugar
- 1 tablespoon butter, melted
- 2 eggs, beaten
- ¼ cup golden raisins, or 1 tablespoon chopped fresh parsley

COOK'S TIP
SMALLER KNISHES CAN BE MADE BY USING A 3-INCH ROUND CUTTER AND CUTTING CIRCLES FROM DOUGH. FOLD OVER 1 SPOONFUL OF FILLING TO MAKE A HALF-MOON SHAPE AND PROCEED AS ABOVE.

POTATO FILLING
FRY 1 FINELY CHOPPED ONION IN 1 TABLESPOON CHICKEN FAT, BUTTER OR MARGARINE. STIR IN 2 CUPS MASHED POTATOES. REMOVE FROM HEAT, COOL SLIGHTLY. BEAT IN 1 EGG AND SALT AND PEPPER TO TASTE, COOL BEFORE USING.

PERUVIAN PICKLED FISH

4 TO 6 SERVINGS

This very contemporary fish dish, also known as ceviche, is popular with Jews in Central and South America. Any firm white fish can be used, as well as salmon, sea trout and even thinly sliced scallops. The acid in the lime and lemon juice has a similar effect to heat; the fish is effectively cooked.

- 2 pounds sole, halibut or red snapper fillets, or any combination of firm-fleshed, non-oily fish
- 1 cup fresh lemon juice
- 1 cup fresh lime juice
- 2 red chilis, thinly sliced
- 2 red onions, thinly sliced
- 1 to 2 garlic cloves, peeled and finely chopped
- Kosher salt to taste
- Freshly ground black pepper to taste
- Fresh coriander leaves for garnish

☐ Cut fish fillets into 1-inch strips; place in a large, shallow nonmetalic dish.

☐ In a large bowl, combine the remaining ingredients, except garnish. Pour marinade over the fish strips, spreading evenly over fish. Refrigerate at least 3 hours, or until the fish strips turn white and opaque. (Do not marinate much longer or the fish will begin to fall apart as the acids continue to break down the proteins.)

☐ Serve a few fish strips with some chili and onion slices on individual plates and garnish with coriander leaves.

BEET BORSHT

6 SERVINGS

There are many versions of borsht; the only ingredient which does not vary is the beet! This soup is made all over Eastern Europe and served hot or cold. It can be made with beef or without, with vegetables or without, and served chunky or smooth.

This elegant ruby-red purée is most delicious served with a swirl of sour cream, snipped chives and dill and for an extra treat, serve with a tiny Piroshki (see page 17) or two.

- 1½ pounds small beets with tops
- 1 onion chopped
- 2 pints beef, chicken or vegetable stock, or water
- 1 teaspoon salt
- Freshly ground black pepper

- 3 tablespoons fresh lemon juice or cider vinegar
- 2 tablespoons light brown sugar, or to taste
- Sour cream for serving
- Snipped fresh chives and dill for garnish

☐ Cut tops from beets, leaving 2 to 3 inches of stem attached. Scrub beets thoroughly under cold running water, being sure to remove all grit and sand. If tops are young and tender they may be added, well washed.

☐ In a large saucepan, over medium heat, place beets and chopped onion and cover with stock or water. Bring to a boil, then simmer, partially covered, until beets are tender, 20 to 30 minutes. Carefully strain liquid into a large heatproof bowl; rinse saucepan.

☐ Remove beets and peel off their skins. Quarter beets and add to a food processor fitted with metal blade. Add onions (and tops if using) from strainer to the beets; process until finely puréed.

☐ Return beet and onion purée to washed saucepan and add reserved cooking liquid, being careful not to add any sand or grit which may have settled on bottom.

☐ Over medium heat, bring soup to a boil. Season with salt, pepper, lemon juice or vinegar and brown sugar. Simmer 5 minutes and serve hot with a swirl of sour cream. Sprinkle with fresh chives and dill. Alternatively, cool and chill to serve cold.

> **COOK'S TIP**
>
> IF SERVING COLD, RESEASON
> BEFORE SERVING AND THIN
> WITH A LITTLE WATER IF
> NECESSARY.

SWEET-AND-SOUR CABBAGE SOUP

8 SERVINGS

The combination of sweet and sour is very popular in Eastern-European Jewish cuisine. Perhaps this is why Jews are so fond of those flavors in Chinese food!

- 2 pounds brisket of beef
- 1 marrow bone (optional if unobtainable)
- 2 onions, chopped
- 2 carrots, finely chopped
- 2 large tomatoes, peeled, seeded, and chopped

- 1 small cabbage, quartered, cored and finely shredded
- ½ cup seedless raisins
- Juice of 2 lemons
- ¼ cup light brown sugar
- Salt
- Freshly ground black pepper

☐ In a large Dutch oven or saucepot, place beef, bone if using, and 2 quarts water. Over medium-high heat, bring to a boil. Skim off any foam which comes to the surface and boil for 5 minutes, skimming as necessary. Reduce heat and simmer 1 hour.

☐ Add chopped onions, carrots and tomatoes and continue cooking until meat is tender, at least 1 hour longer. Remove meat and marrow bone.

☐ Add shredded cabbage and raisins to soup. Cover and simmer until cabbage is just tender, 20 to 30 minutes; add a little water if soup has reduced too much.

☐ Meanwhile, cut or shred meat into small pieces. Discard marrow bone. Add meat pieces to soup with lemon juice, sugar, salt and pepper to taste. Adjust sweet-and-sour balance to your taste. Simmer 10 minutes longer and serve hot.

ABOVE BEET BORSHT.

MUSHROOM AND BARLEY SOUP

8 SERVINGS

Wild mushrooms were easily found in the damp woodlands of Eastern Europe, and this soup is a favorite with Jews from that area. Often made with a beef base, this is a vegetarian version, but either way it is a rich and satisfying soup thickened by the barley and flavored with mushrooms. A little dill sprinkled over the top makes a delicious garnish.

- ½ cup dried mushrooms (see Note)
- 1 tablespoon vegetable oil
- 1 onion, finely chopped
- 2 carrots, finely chopped
- 1 small rutabaga, peeled and finely chopped
- 3 cups chopped button mushrooms
- 1 cup pearl barley
- 1 teaspoon salt
- Freshly ground black pepper
- Chopped fresh dill for garnish

☐ In a small bowl, place dried mushrooms. Cover with hot water and soak for 20 minutes. (Alternatively, follow directions on package.)

☐ Meanwhile, in a large Dutch oven or saucepot, heat oil. Add onion and cook until softened 3 to 5 minutes. Add carrots, rutabaga, button mushrooms and barley. Cover vegetables with cold water.

☐ Over high heat, bring to a boil. Skim off any foam which comes to the surface, reduce heat and simmer until vegetables and barley are just tender, 30 to 35 minutes; you may need to add more water.

☐ Using a slotted spoon, carefully remove dried, soaked mushrooms from their soaking liquid; do not pour liquid over them as any sand will not be left behind. Slice mushrooms and add to soup.

☐ Strain soaking liquid through a cheesecloth-lined strainer and add to soup. Continue cooking more until flavors are blended, 20 to 30 minutes. Serve hot, garnished with chopped fresh dill.

> **NOTE**
>
> USE CÈPE OR PORCINI DRIED MUSHROOMS; DO NOT USE CHINESE OR JAPANESE DRIED MUSHROOMS. CÈPES OR PORCINI ARE OFTEN AVAILABLE DRIED FROM GOURMET SUPERMARKETS AND SPECIALTY STORES. THEY HAVE A STRONGER FLAVOR THAN FRESH MUSHROOMS.

LENTIL SOUP

8 SERVINGS

Jewish folklore claims that this is the soup for which Esau sold his birthright. That may be an exaggeration, but this soup is very popular in Israel and as a warming winter soup throughout Eastern Europe. Use red lentils if you can find them, because the color is rich and tempting and they do not need presoaking. For a pareve soup, use vegetable oil and water or a vegetable stock.

- 2 tablespoons chicken fat
- 2 onions, finely chopped
- 2 stalks celery, finely chopped
- 2 carrots, finely chopped
- 2 cups red or brown lentils (if using brown lentils, follow directions on package for soaking)
- 2 quarts beef broth or water
- Salt
- Freshly ground black pepper
- 1 teaspoon grated nutmeg or ground cloves
- Chopped fresh parsley for garnish

☐ In a large Dutch oven or saucepot, over medium heat, melt chicken fat. Add onions and cook until softened and just beginning to color, 3 to 5 minutes. Add celery, carrots and lentils. Add beef broth and enough water to cover generously.

☐ Bring to a boil and skim off any foam which comes to the surface. Reduce heat, cover and simmer until vegetables and lentils are tender, 45 to 50 minutes, adding a little more water if necessary. (Brown lentils may take longer to cook.)

☐ Into a food processor fitted with metal blade, ladle half the soup. Process until puréed. Return purée to soup. Season with salt and pepper to taste and add grated nutmeg or ground cloves. Serve hot, garnished with chopped parsley.

CLASSIC CHICKEN SOUP WITH MATZO BALLS

8 TO 10 SERVINGS

Chicken soup, also known as "Jewish pencillin" is thought by Jewish mothers to cure all ills! It is a simple soup made all over the world and the seasonings used reflect its regional origins. Matzo balls are one of the most popular accompaniments but noodles, rice, tiny matzo squares, flour-based dumplings (kreplach), can all be added.

- 1 large boiling fowl, about 5 pounds, quartered (ask butcher to include giblets, neck and feet, but not livers)
- 3 carrots, cut into pieces
- 2 medium onions, a few skins reserved
- 2 stalks celery
- 3 leeks, split and well rinsed
- 1 ripe tomato, quartered and pipped
- 2 garlic cloves, peeled
- 2 chicken bouillon cubes (optional)
- 1 tablespoon black peppercorns
- 1 teaspoon salt
- Stems from 1 small bunch fresh parsley

- Chopped fresh parsley for garnish

MATZO BALLS
(KNEIDLACH)

- 1 cup medium matzo meal
- ½ teaspoon salt
- ½ teaspoon freshly ground black pepper
- ¼ teaspoon ground ginger
- ¼ teaspoon ground cinnamon
- 1 cup boiling water
- 2 tablespoons blanched almonds, very finely ground
- 2 tablespoons chicken fat or soft margarine
- 1 egg, lightly beaten

☐ Remove any excess fat from inside and outside of chicken. (Chicken fat can be discarded or rendered for schmaltz, see page 14). Remove any yellow or green bits from giblets. Place chicken pieces, giblets, neck and feet in a large bowl. Pour over boiling water; drain. Scrape off any hard skin from feet.

☐ Place chicken pieces, neck and feet in a large stockpot and cover with cold water. Over high heat, bring to a boil, then skim any foam which comes to the surface. Add giblets and remaining soup ingredients, except parsley for garnish, and bring to a boil, skimming any more foam which comes to surface. Reduce heat to low and simmer about 3 hours.

☐ Strain soup into a large heatproof bowl, reserving chicken pieces and giblets. Cool soup, then refrigerate, covered, overnight. Remove meat from the chicken bones and cut into small pieces. Cut giblets into small pieces and add to chicken pieces. Refrigerate, covered, overnight.

☐ Prepare matzo balls. In a large bowl, mix matzo meal with salt, pepper, ginger and cinnamon. Pour boiling water over and stir. Add finely ground almonds, chicken fat or soft margarine and beaten egg. Mix and refrigerate at least 2 hours.

☐ To serve, remove cold soup from refrigerator and carefully remove any congealed fat from the surface. Transfer to a large saucepot, add cut-up chicken and giblets and bring to a boil.

☐ Remove matzo-ball mixture from refrigerator. Scoop out mixture and form into 1-inch balls, rolling mixture between wet palms of hands. Drop balls into simmering soup and cook until matzo balls are floating and puffed, 20 to 30 minutes. Do not let soup boil or balls will fall apart.

☐ Stir in chopped fresh parsley and serve immediately.

ABOVE FRESH FRUIT AND VEGETABLES FOR SALE IN MINORCA, SPAIN.

ITALIAN BEAN AND PASTA SOUP

6 SERVINGS

Bean soups are popular with most Jewish communities. Ashkenazic and Sephardic seasonings vary but chunky, flavorful soups are always welcome as a first course or light meal. This Jewish–Italian soup is scented with sage, rosemary and basil.

- 1½ cups dried navy or cannellini beans, soaked at least 8 hours
- 2 tablespoons olive oil
- 1 onion, finely chopped
- 1 stalk celery, finely chopped
- 1 carrot, finely chopped
- 1 pound fresh tomatoes, peeled, seeded and chopped, or 1 28-ounce can plum tomatoes, drained and chopped
- 3 to 4 garlic cloves, peeled and crushed
- 2 chicken or vegetable bouillon cubes, crumbled
- 2 bay leaves
- 2 teaspoons dried rosemary, crumbled
- 1 teaspoon dried sage, crumbled
- 1 cup small pasta shapes, such as shells, bows or wheels
- 3 tablespoons chopped fresh parsley
- 3 tablespoons shredded fresh basil leaves
- Salt
- Freshly ground black pepper
- Fresh basil leaves for garnish

☐ Drain soaked beans. In a large Dutch oven or saucepot, combine beans and 1 quart water. Over high heat, bring to a boil. Skim off any foam which comes to the surface, reduce heat and simmer until beans are tender, 1 to 1½ hours. Add water occasionally so beans remain covered. Remove from heat.

☐ In another large saucepot, over medium heat, heat olive oil. Add chopped onion and cook until onion begins to soften, 4 to 5 minutes. Add chopped celery and chopped carrot and continue cooking 4 to 5 minutes longer. Add chopped tomatoes, garlic, bouillon cubes, bay leaves, rosemary and sage and bring to a boil.

☐ Cook, uncovered, until vegetables are tender, about 5 minutes. Add cooked beans and 1 quart cooking liquid (make up liquid with water, if necessary).

☐ Bring soup to a boil. Add pasta and cook, uncovered, until pasta is tender, 8 to 10 minutes. Stir in chopped parsley and shredded basil. Season with salt and freshly ground black pepper. Garnish each portion with a fresh basil leaf.

SHCHAV

8 SERVINGS

This is a Russian soup made from sorrel, also called "sour grass," which is generally served cold. Sorrel can be difficult to find unless you are lucky enough to grow it in your garden, but young spinach leaves make a good substitute, although they lack the sharpness of the sorrel leaves. This soup was frequently served on Shavuot.

- 1 pound sorrel or young spinach leaves, well rinsed and coarsely chopped
- 1 bunch watercress, chopped
- 1 onion, chopped
- 1 stalk celery, finely chopped
- 2 quarts vegetable stock (optional)
- Juice and grated zest of 1 lemon
- 2 or 3 tablespoons sugar
- Salt
- Freshly ground black pepper
- Sour cream and fresh dill sprigs for garnish

☐ Into a large Dutch oven or saucepot, place sorrel or spinach, watercress, onion and celery. Pour in 2 quarts vegetable stock or water. Over high heat, bring to a boil, then simmer partially covered, 20 minutes, until watercress is just tender. Cool slightly.

☐ Into a blender or food processor, ladle soup. Blend or process until finely puréed. Return soup to pot and add lemon juice and zest, sugar, salt and pepper to taste. Pour into a nonmetalic container and cool completely. Refrigerate at least 3 to 4 hours or until ready to serve.

☐ Serve Shchav chilled in chilled bowls, topped with a dollop of sour cream and sprig of dill.

ABOVE ITALIAN BEAN AND PASTA SOUP.

Egg Dishes, Blintzes and Pancakes

Haminados

Egg and Onion

Scrambled Eggs with Lox

Matzo Brei

Orange-Challah French Toast

Blinis with Smoked Salmon
and Sour Cream

Cheese Blintzes with Strawberries

Persian Pancakes with Yogurt

HAMINADOS

8 SERVINGS

These slow-cooked eggs are a typical Sephardic Passover dish. They are sometimes cooked in a stew, such as hamin or dfina, but are simple to do on their own. Serve as an appetizer, sliced in salads or at barbecues or picnics with hummus. The onion skins give the eggs their golden-brown color.

- 8 large eggs
- Skins of 8 onions
- 1 teaspoon salt
- ½ teaspoon freshly ground
- black pepper
- 2 tablespoons olive oil
- Hummus for serving (see page 24)

☐ Preheat oven to 350°F. Into a small ovenproof casserole, place all ingredients, except hummus; add enough water to cover. Cover tightly and place in the oven. Immediately reduce heat to minimum, about 200°F, and bake for 6 to 8 hours or overnight.

☐ Rinse and drain eggs. They can be served warm or chilled with a little hummus on the side.

EGG AND ONION

6 SERVINGS

This simple egg dish is a favorite appetizer, especially with English Jews. It is often served with chopped liver, a scoop of each, as a simple, easy-to-do appetizer for a Sabbath dinner, or used as a sandwich filling. It can be made with raw or cooked onions, or scallions which have a milder flavor. It is delicious with rye or black bread. This is my neighbor's recipe. She serves it with matzos.

- 1 large onion, quartered
- 8 eggs, hard-boiled and quartered
- 2 to 3 tablespoons chicken fat, soft margarine or chicken-flavored vegetable fat
- Salt
- Freshly ground black pepper
- Fresh parsley sprigs for garnish

☐ In a food processor fitted with metal blade, place onion. Process until finely chopped. Replace metal blade with plastic blade, and add egg quarters and chicken fat or margarine. Using pulse action, process until coarsely chopped but well blended. Do not overprocess. Season with salt and pepper and process 2 to 3 seconds.

☐ Turn into a serving dish and refrigerate until ready to serve. Garnish with parsley before serving.

> **COOK'S TIP**
>
> SERVE IN SCOOPS WITH
> STRIPS OF SMOKED SALMON
> OR LOX TO GARNISH.

SCRAMBLED EGGS WITH LOX

4 SERVINGS

This is a favorite brunch dish which is easily prepared ahead and then cooked at the last minute. Small pieces of lox or smoked salmon are often available at Jewish delis at a reasonable price, and a little goes a long way in this dish. Other smoked fish, such as whitefish, sturgeon or haddock, can be substituted.

- 4 tablespoons butter or margarine
- 1 large onion, cut in half and thinly sliced
- 10 large eggs
- Salt
- Freshly ground black pepper
- ½ pound lox or smoked salmon, diced
- Fresh parsley sprigs for garnish

☐ In a large skillet, over a medium-low heat, melt 2 tablespoons butter or margarine. Add onion and cook until softened and lightly golden, 8 to 10 minutes.

☐ In a large bowl, whisk eggs with salt and pepper to taste. Melt remaining butter or margarine in skillet with onions and add egg mixture. Reduce heat to low and scramble eggs gently, stirring constantly.

☐ Just before eggs are set, gently stir in diced lox or smoked salmon. Serve immediately, garnished with parsley.

MATZO BREI

Matzo brei is a dairy dish which is kosher for Passover. It is quick and easy, and the children love it. Serve with applesauce and sour cream.

- 2 whole matzos
- ½ cup milk or water
- 2 eggs, well beaten
- Salt
- Freshly ground black pepper
- ¼ teaspoon ground cinnamon (optional)

- 2 tablespoons butter or pareve margarine
- Sugar and ground cinnamon for sprinkling
- Applesauce and sour cream for serving

☐ Into a large shallow bowl, break matzos into small pieces. Pour over milk or water and leave to stand until matzos softened and milk partly absorbed, about 5 minutes.

☐ Beat in eggs, salt and pepper to taste and cinnamon if using.

☐ In a medium skillet, over medium heat, melt butter or margarine. Add egg and matzo mixture and cover. Cook until underside is golden brown, 10 minutes. With a metal pancake turner, carefully turn over and cook 3 minutes longer or until brown. Serve in wedges with a sprinkling of sugar and cinnamon. Accompany it with applesauce and sour cream.

ORANGE-CHALLAH FRENCH TOAST

6 SERVINGS

My favorite recipe for French toast. The challah should be cut quite thick and left to soak in the egg mixture so that when it is cooked the outside is brown and crisp but the inside remains soft and moist. Serve with maple syrup or dust with confectioners' sugar.

- 4 eggs, well beaten
- ½ teaspoon salt
- 2 tablespoons sugar
- 1 cup orange juice
- ½ teaspoon vanilla extract
- ½ to 1 cup milk
- 12 slices challah bread, each about ¾ inch thick

- Butter for frying, melted
- Maple syrup or confectioners' sugar for serving
- Orange slices for garnish (optional)

☐ In a large shallow baking dish, beat eggs with salt, sugar, orange juice, vanilla and ½ cup milk. (Depending on the size of the bread, you may need to add a little more milk.)

☐ Lay slices of bread in egg mixture and leave to stand 2 minutes. Turn bread slices over and leave to soak until egg mixture is completely absorbed, about 5 minutes longer.

☐ In a large skillet or on a griddle, over medium heat, melt 3 tablespoons butter. Add slices of soaked bread and cook until underside is golden brown, 3 to 5 minutes. Using a metal pancake turner, turn bread slices and cook until brown, 1 to 2 minutes longer.

☐ Serve immediately with maple syrup or confectioners' sugar. Garnish with orange slices.

BLINIS WITH SMOKED SALMON AND SOUR CREAM

6 SERVINGS

Blinis are Russian pancakes made with buckwheat flour. They have a nutty flavor which is enhanced by smoked salmon or lox and sour cream. A less extravagant presentation can be offered with chopped radishes and cucumber, scallions and capers. Blinis make a wonderful brunch, light lunch or supper dish.

- ¼ cup lukewarm water
- 1½ teaspoons active-dry yeast
- ½ cup all-purpose flour
- ¾ cup buckwheat flour
- ½ teaspoon salt
- 1 cup milk
- 2 eggs, separated
- ¼ cup (½ stick) butter or margarine
- 4 scallions, thinly sliced on the diagonal
- ½ cup sour cream
- Snipped fresh chives for garnish

- 2 tablespoons sour cream
- ¼ pound smoked salmon or lox, thinly sliced

COOK'S TIP

BLINIS CAN BE MADE USING ALL-PURPOSE FLOUR, BUT THE FLAVOR AND TEXTURE IS MUCH BETTER USING BUCKWHEAT FLOUR. IT IS AVAILABLE IN HEALTH-FOOD STORES AND SPECIALTY SUPERMARKETS.

☐ Into a small bowl, pour lukewarm water and sprinkle yeast over water. Leave to stand until yeast becomes foamy and bubbly, 5 minutes.

☐ Into a large bowl, sift all-purpose flour, buckwheat flour and salt; make a well in center. Heat ¾ cup of the milk to lukewarm and add it to well with yeast mixture, stirring with a wire whisk and drawing in flour little by little to form a smooth batter. Cover bowl with a clean dish towel and leave in a warm place until the batter becomes light and bubbly, 2 to 3 hours.

☐ Beat remaining ¼ cup milk into batter; beat egg yolks and stir into batter with half butter, melted, and sour cream.

☐ In another bowl, with a hand-held mixer at medium speed, beat egg whites until stiff peaks form (do not overbeat). Fold egg whites into blini batter until just blended. (Do not overblend; a few white lumps will cook out.)

☐ In a large skillet or on a griddle, over medium-high heat, melt remaining butter. Using a small ladle, pour batter into pan or griddle to form small pancakes. Cook until undersides are lightly browned and tops are covered with bubbles, about 2 minutes. Turn blinis over and cook 1 to 2 minutes longer. Continue until all batter is used, adding more butter if necessary. (Keep blinis warm in a 300°F oven if necessary.)

☐ Arrange blinis on individual plates or on a large serving dish. Divide smoked salmon or lox slices equally on to blinis. Top each blini with a few sliced scallions and a spoonful of sour cream. Sprinkle with chives and serve warm.

ABOVE BLINIS WITH SMOKED SALMON AND SOUR CREAM.

CHEESE BLINTZES WITH STRAWBERRIES

6 TO 8 SERVINGS

Blintzes are a symbol of Jewish cooking around the world, with the name coming from the Yiddish for pancake. It is a simple crêpe or pancake filled with cheese or fruits or savory fillings such as potato and mushroom, chicken livers, cabbage or meat. The blintze, filled with cheese and topped with fruit is a staple meal in Jewish dairy restaurants and makes an ideal choice for a milk meal at Passover, Shavuot or any time.

- 3 large eggs
- ½ teaspoon salt
- ½ teaspoon sugar
- 2 tablespoons butter or margarine, melted
- 1½ cups milk or water
- ⅔ cup all-purpose flour
- Butter or margarine for baking or frying, melted

FILLING
- 1 16-ounce container creamed cottage cheese
- 2 3-ounce package cream cheese, softened
- ¼ cup sugar
- 1 teaspoon vanilla extract
- 1 pound strawberries, thawed if frozen
- Sugar
- Juice and grated zest of 1 lemon

☐ In a large bowl, beat eggs, salt, sugar, melted butter or margarine and milk or water until well blended.

☐ Into a medium bowl, sift flour; make a well in center. Using a wire whisk, gradually stir beaten egg mixture into flour, drawing in flour from edges of well until all egg mixture is added. Whisk until smooth. Strain into a 4-cup measure. Cover and refrigerate about 1 hour. (Batter may thicken; add milk or water to thin if necessary.)

☐ Over medium heat, heat a 7-inch crêpe pan or skillet. Brush bottom of pan with a little melted butter. Pour 3 to 4 tablespoons (about ¼ cup) batter into crêpe pan, tipping pan to coat bottom with batter. Cook until top looks set and bottom is lightly browned, about 2 minutes. Using a metal pancake turner, loosen edges and flip crêpe, then cook 10 seconds. Slip cooked blintze on to a piece of waxed paper. Repeat until all batter is used, stacking blintzes between sheets of waxed paper. (Blintzes can be used immediately or stored in the refrigerator or frozen.)

☐ Preheat oven to 350°F. Brush a 15½- × 10½-inch jelly-roll pan with melted butter or margarine.

☐ Make filling. In a medium bowl, with a mixer at medium speed, beat cottage cheese, cream cheese, sugar and vanilla until smooth.

☐ On a clean work surface, spread 1 heaped tablespoon of cheese mixture down center of each blintze. Fold sides toward center, so each side covers about half the filling. Beginning at bottom edge, roll up blintze. Arrange seam-side down on buttered pan. Brush each folded blintze with a little butter and bake until heated through, about 10 minutes.

☐ Reserve 6 to 8 strawberries and hull remainder. Slice each in half lengthwise and set aside. Into a food processor, fitted with metal blade, place half remaining strawberries. Add sugar to taste and lemon juice and grated zest. Process until smooth and pour into small bowl. Chop remaining strawberries and add to purée. Add more sugar if necessary.

☐ To serve, place 2 blintzes on a plate, spoon over a little strawberry sauce and garnish with a strawberry half.

> **NOTE**
>
> FOR PASSOVER, THE BLINTZE BATTER
> CAN BE MADE WITH POTATO FLOUR AND
> WATER. THE MIXTURE WILL BE SLIGHTLY
> THINNER AND WILL MAKE A CRISPER
> BLINTZE.

PERSIAN PANCAKES WITH YOGURT

4 SERVINGS

My friend Sheema comes from the border area of Pakistan and Iran. She makes these delicious "green" pancakes which are like a fritter. They can be eaten on their own with yogurt or cream cheese, or as an accompaniment to spicy curries, which is how she often serves them.

- 4 cups chopped spinach, Swiss chard or watercress
- 2 large sprigs each fresh coriander, parsley and dill
- 2 small leeks, or 4 large scallions, thinly sliced
- 6 eggs, beaten
- Salt
- Freshly ground black pepper
- ¼ teaspoon grated nutmeg
- 1 cup matzo meal
- Vegetable oil for frying
- Yogurt, sour cream or cream cheese for serving
- Fresh coriander or dill for garnish

☐ In a food procesor fitted with metal blade, process spinach, Swiss chard or watercress, herbs and leeks or scallions until smooth. Turn into a large bowl. Add beaten eggs, salt and pepper to taste and nutmeg. Stir in matzo meal. Batter should be quite thick but pourable.

☐ In a large skillet, over high heat, heat 2 tablespoons oil. Drop batter by heaping tablespoonsful into pan. Cook until undersides are lightly browned, about 2 minutes, then turn over and cook 2 minutes longer. Remove to paper towels to drain; keep warm. Continue until all batter is used, adding more oil to skillet as needed. (Keep warm in a 300°F oven until all batter is used.) Serve hot with yogurt, sour cream or cream cheese, garnished with coriander or dill.

POULTRY AND MEAT DISHES

SPICED ROAST CHICKEN WITH
MATZO STUFFING

ROAST GOOSE WITH FRUITY STUFFING

SPICY BARBECUED CHICKEN

CHICKEN WITH WALNUTS AND POMEGRANATES

ISRAELI ROAST DUCK

NORTH AFRICAN-STYLE ROCK CORNISH HENS

COCHIN-STYLE CHILI CHICKEN

SPICY TURKEY SCHNITZEL

INDIAN-JEWISH CHICKEN

SENIYEH

BEEF TONGUE WITH SWEET-AND-SOUR SAUCE

MEXICAN BEEF TZIMMES

HAMIN

SWEET-AND-SOUR STUFFED CABBAGE

OLD-FASHIONED POT ROAST WITH ONION GRAVY

CHOLENT

SHASHLIK

STUFFED PASSOVER LAMB

SPICED ROAST CHICKEN WITH MATZO STUFFING

4 SERVINGS

My sister-in-law prepares this matzo stuffing during Passover, but I find it delicious enough to use anytime. She does not flavor her chicken with cumin and turmeric, typical of Morocco, Tunisia and other Middle Eastern countries, but I think the combination is a great success.

MATZO STUFFING
- 2 to 3 matzos, broken into small pieces
- ½ cup chicken soup, stock or water, heated
- 1 tablespoon olive or vegetable oil
- 1 large onion, chopped
- 2 stalks celery, finely chopped
- Salt
- Freshly ground black pepper
- ½ teaspoon ground cumin (optional)
- ¼ teaspoon turmeric (optional)

- 1 tablespoon chopped fresh parsley
- 1 egg, beaten

- 1 3½- to 4-pound roasting chicken
- 1 lemon, cut in half
- Salt
- Freshly ground black pepper
- 1 teaspoon ground cumin
- ¼ teaspoon ground turmeric
- 1 tablespoon olive oil
- 1 onion, thinly sliced
- Fresh parsley sprigs for garnish

☐ Prepare stuffing. Into a large bowl, place broken matzos. Pour hot chicken soup, stock or water over them and leave to stand until liquid is absorbed.

☐ In a large skillet, over medium heat, heat oil. Add onion and celery and cook until vegetables begin to soften, 3 to 4 minutes. Add salt and pepper to taste and sprinkle in the cumin and turmeric, if using. Cook, stirring frequently, until mixture is golden, 4 to 5 minutes. Stir in matzo mixture. Remove from heat and leave to cool. Stir in chopped parsley and beaten egg.

☐ Preheat oven to 400°F. Remove any excess fat from chicken and cavity. Wash under cold running water and pat dry with paper towels. Rub outside of chicken all over with lemon half; squeeze other half into cavity. Season chicken with salt and pepper to taste and cumin and turmeric. Rub or brush olive oil over.

☐ Spoon stuffing into bird and close with skewers or toothpicks if necessary. Place sliced onion in a medium roasting pan and lay the chicken on top. Roast, basting with the pan juices occasionally, for 1¼ to 1½ hours. Halfway through roasting time, add ½ to 1 cup water to dissolve juices. Chicken is cooked through when juices run clear when leg is pierced with a knife or skewer.

☐ Transfer chicken to carving board and cover loosely with foil. Leave to rest in a warm place for 10 to 15 minutes.

☐ Pour any pan juices and onion into a small saucepan. Heat to boiling and reduce slightly, skimming any foam which comes to the surface. Pour into a gravy boat. Place chicken on serving platter, garnished with parsley. If you like, remove stuffing to a separate bowl for easier serving.

ROAST GOOSE WITH FRUITY STUFFING

6 TO 8 SERVINGS

Goose was so important in 16th-century Jewish cooking that it was known as the "Jew's fowl" in Germany: not only was the meat eaten, the fat rendered and used as the staple cooking fat, but the quills and down were sold and the liver used for liver pâté. Today, Israel is one of the world's main producers of geese and goose liver. In Northern European countries, goose is often roasted stuffed with apples or an apple-based stuffing. This fruity stuffing can be baked in a dish alongside the goose if you prefer; roast potatoes (in goose fat, of course!) make the perfect accompaniment.

- 1 8- to 10-pound young goose, thawed if frozen
- Salt
- Freshly ground black pepper
- 1 tablespoon vegetable oil
- 1 large onion, chopped
- 6 to 8 sharp apples, peeled, cored and cut up
- ½ cup raisins
- 1 cup chopped pitted prunes
- ½ cup chopped no-soak dried apricots
- 1 15½- to 16-ounce can cooked peeled chestnuts packed in water, drained
- ½ teaspoon crumbled dried sage
- 1 tablespoon chopped fresh parsley
- 1 tablespoon potatostarch
- ½ cup apple juice
- 1 tablespoon cider vinegar
- Watercress and apple slices for garnish

☐ Remove all excess fat from inside and outside goose (discard or render for cooking fat). Cut off fatty skin flap near tail. Rub skin and sprinkle cavity with salt and pepper. Prick skin all over with a fork to let fat escape during roasting.

☐ In a large skillet, over medium-high heat, heat vegetable oil. Add onion and cook until softened, 4 to 5 minutes. Add apples, raisins, prunes, apricots and chestnuts and sprinkle with sage and parsley. Stir in 2 tablespoons water and cook just until liquid evaporates, 2 to 3 minutes. Remove from heat and cool slightly.

☐ Preheat oven to 450°F. Spoon stuffing into goose cavity and close with skewers or sew with kitchen string. Place goose on its back in a large roasting pan and roast 30 minutes.

☐ Reduce oven to 350°F. Remove goose from oven, pour off any fat and prick goose all over again. Turn goose on to its breast and roast for 1½ hours longer, removing fat from the pan and basting 3 or 4 more times. When no more fat is being released, add 1 cup water to roasting pan and continue roasting until goose tests done; juices should run slightly yellow or clear when leg is pierced with a knife or skewer.

☐ When goose is done, remove to a serving platter; cover with foil and leave to rest 20 minutes in a warm place. If you like, remove stuffing to a separate bowl.

☐ Pour off all but 1 tablespoon fat from the pan drippings. Stir potatostarch, apple juice and vinegar together and add to pan with ½ cup water, adding more water if necessary. Season with salt and pepper to taste. Bring to a boil, stirring and scraping up any bits from the pan. Reduce heat and simmer 5 minutes. Strain into a gravy boat.

☐ Arrange watercress and sliced apples around the goose and serve the gravy separately.

BELOW SHABBAT CHICKEN, ARGENTINIAN-STYLE.

SPICY BARBECUED CHICKEN

6 TO 8 SERVINGS

Barbecued foods are even more popular in Israel than the United States and the variety is amazing. No street corner is without an open fire covered with skewers of meat, chicken, chicken hearts and vegetables and patties of all kinds. Try this easy recipe using chicken. Serve with lots of potato salad and Israeli Salad (see pages 91 and 89).

- 4 to 5 pounds chicken pieces
- 2 tablespoons olive oil
- 2 tablespoons ground cumin
- 1½ teaspoons turmeric
- 1 teaspoon hot or mild paprika or chili powder
- Fresh coriander leaves for garnish

☐ Rub chicken pieces with olive oil. Arrange on a cookie sheet and sprinkle spices equally over both sides. Leave to stand while preparing a barbecue.

☐ Position barbecue rack about 5 inches above preheated coals. Arrange any legs and thighs on rack and cook 10 minutes. Add any breast pieces to rack and cook 7 to 10 minutes longer. Raise rack if chicken browns too quickly.

☐ Turn chicken pieces over and cook breast pieces 7 to 10 minutes longer and legs and thigh pieces 12 to 15 minutes longer, or until juices run clear when pieces are pierced with a knife or skewer.

☐ Arrange chicken pieces on a large serving platter and garnish with coriander leaves.

COOK'S TIP

LAMB CUBES CAN BE COOKED
THE SAME WAY.

CHICKEN WITH WALNUTS AND POMEGRANATES

4 SERVINGS

Pomegranates are one of the most symbolic fruits in Jewish history. They are significant for Rosh Hashanah, the New Year, and some Jewish communities even use pomegranate seeds in their Passover haroset. This braised chicken with walnuts and pomegranates is one of the most prized dishes among Iranian Jews. Serve with Chelou, a Persian-style rice (see page 86).

- 1 3½-4-pound roasting chicken
- Salt
- Freshly ground black pepper
- 2 tablespoons vegetable oil
- 1 onion, finely chopped
- 2 cups ground or finely chopped walnuts
- 2 cups pomegranate juice, or ½ cup syrup diluted with 1½ cups water
- 2 tablespoons lemon juice
- ⅓ cup boiling water

- 1 tablespoon tomato paste
- 2 cinnamon sticks
- 2 tablespoons light brown sugar
- Watercress, pomegranate seeds and walnut halves for garnish

> **NOTE**
>
> POMEGRANATE JUICE IS AVAILABLE IN MIDDLE EASTERN FOOD STORES.

☐ Rinse chicken under cold running water and dry inside and out with paper towels. Season skin and cavity with salt and pepper.

☐ In a large Dutch oven or heavy deep skillet, over medium-high heat, heat oil. Add chicken and cook until golden brown, turning frequently to allow all sides to brown, 10 to 15 minutes. Remove to a large plate and set aside.

☐ Into pan, stir onion. Cook until beginning to soften, 2 to 3 minutes. Stir in ground or chopped walnuts and cook until well browned, 2 to 3 minutes. Pour in pomegranate juice or syrup mixture, lemon juice and boiling water. Stir in tomato paste, cinnamon sticks and brown sugar and bring just to a boil. Reduce heat to low.

☐ Return chicken to pot and cook, covered, until chicken is tender and juices run clear when leg is pierced with a knife or skewer, 45 to 50 minutes. Remove chicken to a serving platter and cover with foil to keep warm. If sauce is too thin, bring sauce up to a boil and reduce until thickened slightly.

☐ Pour sauce over chicken, garnish platter with watercress and pomegranate seeds and arrange walnut halves over top.

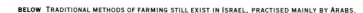

BELOW TRADITIONAL METHODS OF FARMING STILL EXIST IN ISRAEL, PRACTISED MAINLY BY ARABS.

ISRAELI ROAST DUCK

4 SERVINGS

New breeds of duck are being bred in Israel for both eating and for the production of foie gras for liver pâté. The combination of orange and sugar makes a lovely glaze, but grapefruit juice can also be used. A simple gravy can be served with the duck, or it can be served with applesauce and Latkes (see page 73).

- 1 5- to 6-pound duckling, thawed if frozen
- Salt
- Freshly ground black pepper
- ½ orange, quartered
- 1 tablespoon light brown sugar
- ¾ cup fresh orange juice
- 1 onion, thinly sliced
- 1 carrot, thinly sliced
- 1 tablespoon all-purpose flour
- ¾ cup chicken stock or water
- 1 tablespoon cider or distilled white vinegar
- 1 tablespoon orange marmalade
- Fresh parsley sprigs for garnish

☐ Rinse the duck under cold running water. Pat it dry inside and out with paper towels. Remove any excess fat from outside or inside the cavity. Sprinkle cavity with salt and pepper and rub skin with salt and pepper. Prick skin all over with a fork to let fat escape. Place orange quarters in cavity.

☐ In a small bowl, mix brown sugar and 1 teaspoon salt with 3 to 4 tablespoons orange juice. Reserve remaining juice.

☐ Preheat oven to 350°F. Place the sliced onion and carrot into roasting pan; place duck on a rack on top. Roast duck 30 minutes. Remove from oven and baste duck. Pour off fat and prick skin all over again.

☐ Continue roasting duck, basting it and pouring off fat every 20 minutes, until duck is well browned and skin is crisp, 1½ hours. The juices should run clear when upper leg is pierced with a sharp knife or skewer.

☐ Remove duck to a serving platter, cover with foil and leave to stand 15 minutes.

☐ Pour off all but 1 tablespoon fat from pan. Stir in flour. Cook, stirring and scraping the dripping from the pan, 1 to 2 minutes. Stir in remaining orange juice, chicken stock or water, cider or vinegar and marmalade. Bring to a boil and simmer until well blended and thickened, 3 to 4 minutes.

☐ Pour gravy into a gravy boat and serve separately. Garnish duck with parsley and serve quartered or carve at the table.

NORTH AFRICAN-STYLE ROCK CORNISH HENS

4 SERVINGS

Couscous is a popular grain in Morocco and Tunisia and makes an ideal base for a poultry stuffing. Here it is combined with typical North African spices and used to stuff the popular Rock Cornish hen. It can be used to stuff a whole chicken or baked on its own.

- 4 tablespoons olive oil
- 1 small onion, finely chopped
- 2 garlic cloves, peeled and finely chopped
- ¾-inch piece fresh ginger root, finely chopped
- ½ cup pecan halves, toasted and coarsely chopped
- 1⅓ cups quick-cooking couscous
- Salt
- Freshly ground black pepper
- ½ teaspoon cinnamon
- ⅓ cup golden raisins
- ½ cup chopped no-soak dried apricots
- 4 tablespoons chopped fresh mint, or 1 tablespoon dried
- 1 cup tomato juice
- 1 cup boiling water
- 4 Rock Cornish hens
- ½ teaspoon ground ginger
- ½ teaspoon hot paprika
- Fresh parsley sprigs or watercress for garnish

☐ In a large skillet, over medium-high heat, heat 2 tablespoons olive oil. Add onion and cook 2 to 3 minutes. Stir in garlic and ginger root and cook 1 minute longer; add pecans and stir.

☐ Add couscous with salt and pepper to taste, cinnamon, golden raisins, apricots and mint. Stir well to blend. Pour in the tomato juice and water, shaking pan to distribute ingredients evenly. Remove from heat and leave to stand 5 minutes. Remove cover and fluff stuffing mixture with a fork. Cool and taste for seasoning.

☐ Preheat oven to 375°F. Rinse hens under cold running water and pat dry with paper towels. Rub hens with remaining olive oil; sprinkle cavity with salt and pepper and rub ginger and paprika into the skin.

☐ Spoon about 1 cup stuffing mixture into each bird and tie legs with string. Cover remaining stuffing mixture loosely and set aside. Lightly grease a large roasting pan and arrange hens in pan.

☐ Roast birds until crisp and golden and juices run clear when a leg is pierced with a knife or skewer, about 1 hour.

☐ Remove Rock Cornish hens to a serving platter and cover with foil. Add ¼ cup water to roasting pan and stir, scraping up any bits on bottom of pan. Uncover remaining couscous mixture and pour in pan juices. Reheat couscous mixture over medium-low heat 2 to 3 minutes, stirring and fluffing with a fork. Spoon into a serving dish and garnish with a few parsley sprigs or watercress. Serve hens garnished with parsley or watercress.

BELOW FRESH, SUCCULENT FRUIT IS AN IMPORTANT PART OF THE TYPICAL LEVANTINE DIET.

COCHIN-STYLE CHILI CHICKEN

4 SERVINGS

This recipe is based on a dish which comes from the Jewish community in Cochin, in southern India. I have toned down the "heat" somewhat as the original quantity of chilies would be too strong for the average taste. This makes a change from the ordinary braised chicken dish and, as it can be kept warm, makes an ideal choice for a Friday night supper, which is when it is often served in Cochin. Hot boiled rice is the ideal accompaniment.

- 2 tablespoons lemon juice
- 1 teaspoon salt
- 2 tablespoons sugar
- 2 tablespoons vegetable oil
- 10 to 12 fresh or dried curry leaves, or 1 teaspoon curry powder
- 2 cups finely sliced shallots
- 6 garlic cloves, finely chopped
- 1-inch piece fresh ginger root, finely chopped
- 5 medium-hot green chilis, seeded and very finely sliced
- 2 medium tomatoes, chopped
- ½ teaspoon turmeric
- ¼ teaspoon chili powder
- 1 3- to 3½-pound broiler/fryer chicken, cut into 8 pieces
- 2 tablespoons chopped fresh coriander
- Fresh coriander leaves and lemon wedges for garnish

☐ In a small bowl, place lemon juice, ¼ teaspoon salt and sugar; stir to dissolve. Set aside.

☐ In a Dutch oven or large deep skillet, over medium-high heat, heat oil. Add curry leaves or curry powder and stir until they sizzle, 10 to 15 seconds. Stir in shallots, garlic, ginger, and chilis and cook until the shallots have softened and begin to color, 5 to 7 minutes. Stir in tomatoes, turmeric, chili powder and remaining salt. Cook 3 to 4 minutes longer.

☐ Add chicken to vegetable mixture, moving pieces around to cover with some vegetables. Stir in 1 cup water and bring just to a boil. Reduce heat to low and cook, covered tightly, 20 minutes, stirring once.

☐ Uncover and stir in reserved lemon-juice mixture and chopped coriander. Increase heat to medium and cook, uncovered, until sauce is slightly reduced, basting chicken occasionally with the sauce, about 10 minutes.

☐ Arrange chicken pieces on a serving platter. Pour sauce over and garnish with coriander leaves and lemon wedges.

SPICY TURKEY SCHNITZEL

4 SERVINGS

Israel produces great quantities of turkey and chicken and prepares it in ways usually used for other meats, unavailable or too costly. Veal would be prohibitively expensive, so the old-fashioned veal dish of Wiener schnitzel is made with turkey breast and popular Israeli spices. This is one of the most popular dishes in Israel.

- 1¼ pounds turkey breast, cut into 8 slices about ½ inch thick
- 1 teaspoon ground cumin
- ½ teaspoon turmeric
- ½ teaspoon hot paprika
- ½ teaspoon salt
- Freshly ground black pepper
- ⅛ teaspoon cayenne pepper or chili powder
- ½ cup all-purpose flour
- 2 eggs, beaten
- 1 cup matzo meal, or fine fresh bread crumbs
- Vegetable oil for frying
- Lemon wedges and fresh parsley sprigs for garnish

☐ Place each turkey slice between 2 sheets waxed paper and pound them to flatten as thin as possible.

☐ In a small bowl, combine cumin, turmeric, paprika, salt, pepper to taste and cayenne pepper or chili powder. Rub spice mixture into both sides of turkey slices and leave 30 minutes.

☐ Into 3 pie plates or shallow dishes, place flour, beaten eggs and matzo meal or bread crumbs. Dip each spice-covered turkey slice first into flour to coat, shaking off the excess; then into the egg, brushing to coat completely; then into matzo meal or crumbs. Arrange on a cookie sheet.

☐ In a large skillet or on a griddle, over medium-high heat, heat 2 to 3 tablespoons oil. Add a few turkey slices, but do not allow to overlap. Fry quickly, until underside is golden brown, about 2 minutes, then, using a metal pancake turner, carefully turn slices over. Cook until other side is browned and turkey cooked, 1 to 2 minutes longer. Continue to cook in batches, adding more oil if necessary. Remove to paper towels to drain.

☐ Arrange turkey slices on an ovenproof serving platter and keep warm while cooking remaining slices. Garnish turkey schnitzel with lemon wedges and parsley sprigs.

INDIAN-JEWISH CHICKEN

4 SERVINGS

This is a very aromatic dish, often served in the Bene Israel community of Bombay. It is an ideal Sabbath dish and can easily be prepared and cooked overnight in a crockpot or very low oven.

- 1 3- to 3½-pound broiler/fryer chicken
- ½ cup vegetable oil
- Salt
- Freshly ground black pepper
- 1 onion, cut in half and thinly sliced
- 2 garlic cloves, finely chopped
- 2 bay leaves
- 1 cinnamon stick
- 4 whole cloves
- 4 cardamom pods
- 1 tablespoon curry powder or garam masala
- 1 tablespoon finely chopped or grated ginger root
- ¼ teaspoon turmeric
- 1 cup chicken or vegetable stock or water
- Fresh parsley sprigs for garnish

☐ Rinse chicken under cold running water and pat dry with paper towels. On a cutting board, remove legs and thighs from body and separate drumstick from thigh. Remove wing tips; remove breasts and wings from carcass and cut each breast into 2 pieces; upper breast portion can include wing. This gives you 8 pieces. (Wing tips and carcass can be used for soup.)

☐ Preheat oven to 250°F. In a large Dutch oven or deep skillet with ovenproof lid, over medium-high heat, heat oil. Add chicken pieces, season with salt and pepper and cook until underside is golden, 5 to 7 minutes. Turn chicken pieces and add remaining ingredients, stirring to blend well.

☐ Cover pan tightly and bake, basting occasionally, for 1½ to 2 hours, adding a little more chicken stock or water if all liquid has been absorbed.

☐ To serve, arrange the chicken pieces on a serving platter and pour any juices over; garnish with parsley sprigs.

ABOVE SPICY TURKEY SCHNITZEL.

SENIYEH

4 TO 6 SERVINGS

This traditional Yemenite dish is a kosher version of moussaka, a Greek specialty. Replacing the milk-based béchamel sauce with a tahini topping makes this a great Sabbath supper dish. Serve with mashed potatoes or lots of rice and salad.

- 1 pound lean ground lamb
- 1 tablespoon all-purpose flour
- 2 onions, finely chopped
- 2 garlic cloves, peeled and finely chopped
- 2 tablespoons chopped fresh parsley or coriander
- ½ teaspoon ground cinnamon
- Salt
- Freshly ground black pepper
- ½ teaspoon zhoug (see page 11), or ¼ teaspoon cayenne pepper
- 2 tablespoons olive oil
- ¼ cup pine nuts, toasted
- ½ cup tahini
- 3 to 4 tablespoons lemon juice

☐ Into a large bowl, place meat. Sprinkle with flour and toss to mix. Add onions, garlic, parsley or coriander and cinnamon and mix well. Season with salt and pepper to taste. Stir in the zhoug or cayenne, oil and 2 tablespoons pine nuts.

☐ Preheat oven to 350°F. Lightly oil a shallow 2-quart round baking dish. Spread meat mixture in dish, smoothing top evenly.

☐ In a small bowl, mix tahini, lemon juice and 1 to 2 tablespoons water. Pour over meat mixture and sprinkle with remaining pine nuts.

☐ Cook, uncovered, until top is brown and bubbling and meat is cooked, 35 to 40 minutes. (Knife or skewer should feel hot when inserted into center of meat, held for 30 seconds and then removed.)

BEEF TONGUE WITH SWEET-AND-SOUR SAUCE

6 TO 8 SERVINGS

Tongue has had a special symbolism for Jews since Biblical times, when Abraham prepared a feast for the angels, choosing tongue as one of the gifts. The sweet-and-sour version, particularly popular with German and Polish Jews, is traditional at Sukkot. This is my mother's recipe.

- 1 4-pound beef tongue
- 1 tablespoon distilled white vinegar
- 6 whole cloves
- 1 tablespoon black peppercorns
- 1 bay leaf
- Fresh parsley sprigs for garnish

- ½ cup tomato sauce
- Grated zest and juice of 1 lemon
- 3 tablespoons light brown sugar
- 1 tablespoon honey
- ½ cup seedless raisins

SWEET-AND-SOUR SAUCE

- 1 tablespoon chicken fat, margarine or vegetable oil
- 2 onions, thinly sliced
- 1 tablespoon all-purpose flour
- ½ teaspoon salt
- Freshly ground black pepper
- 1 cinnamon stick
- 3 to 4 whole cloves

COOK'S TIP

PICKLED OR SMOKED TONGUE CAN BE USED FOR THE SAME RECIPE, BUT THE TONGUE SHOULD BE SOAKED FOR SEVERAL HOURS OR OVERNIGHT IN SEVERAL CHANGES OF COLD WATER BEFORE COOKING. OMIT ANY ADDITIONAL SALT IF USING PICKLED OR SMOKED TONGUE.

☐ Into a large stockpot or kettle, place tongue, vinegar, cloves, peppercorns and bay leaf. Cover with cold water and, over high heat, bring to a boil. Skim off any foam which comes to the surface. Boil, skimming often, 5 minutes. Reduce heat to medium-low and simmer until tongue is tender when pierced with a fork, 3 to 4 hours. Add a little water from time to time if necessary to keep tongue covered with liquid.

☐ Remove from heat, but leave tongue to cool in its cooking liquid. When cool, remove tongue from liquid. With a sharp knife, peel off outer skin and the gristle at back of tongue. Set tongue aside. Reserve cooking liquid.

☐ Make sauce. In a large, deep skillet, over medium heat, heat chicken fat, margarine or oil. Add onions and cook until soft and beginning to color, 5 to 7 minutes. Sprinkle onions with flour and cook, stirring constantly, until flour is browned, 1 minute. Slowly add about 2 cups reserved cooking liquid and cook, stirring constantly, until smooth and slightly thickened, about 2 minutes.

☐ Add salt and pepper to taste, then stir in remaining ingredients. Reduce heat to medium-low and simmer, stirring often, 10 minutes. Remove cinnamon stick and cloves.

☐ Slice tongue into ¼-inch slices and add to sauce. Cook until tongue is heated though, 2 to 3 minutes. Arrange tongue slices on a serving platter or directly on individual dinner plates and spoon over a little sauce. Garnish with parsley sprigs.

ABOVE MOROCCAN JEWS STUDYING THE TORAH (THE FIVE BOOKS OF MOSES).

MEXICAN BEEF TZIMMES

8 SERVINGS

A Jewish-Mexican family with whom I once spent a summer in Mexico City had an elderly German-Jewish cook. This is her version of German tzimmes. It combines old-world tradition with new-world ingredients.

Tzimmes is a slowly cooked casserole of meat, sweet vegetables, such as carrots or sweet potatoes, and fruit, most often prunes.

- 3½ pounds boneless beef brisket
- 1½ tablespoons all-purpose flour
- 4 to 6 tablespoons chicken fat *or* vegetable oil
- 2 onions, thinly sliced
- 2 to 4 garlic cloves, peeled
- 1 28-ounce can tomatoes
- 1 large mango, peeled and flesh puréed
- 1 teaspoon salt
- ½ teaspoon dried red-pepper flakes, or to taste

- 1 teaspoon chili powder
- 1 cinnamon stick
- 2 bay leaves
- ¼ cup honey
- 4 carrots, sliced
- 2 large sweet potatoes or yams, peeled and cut into chunks
- 1 cup pitted prunes, soaked in hot water for 2 hours and well drained
- 1 28-ounce can red kidney beans, rinsed and drained
- 4 tablespoons chopped fresh coriander

☐ Rinse beef under cold running water; dry well with paper towels. Dredge meat with flour on both sides.

☐ In a large Dutch oven with tight-fitting lid, over medium-high heat, heat 2 to 3 tablespoons chicken fat or oil. Add beef and cook until underside is well browned, 5 to 7 minutes, turn beef and cook until second side is well browned, 4 to 5 minutes longer. Remove to a plate and set aside.

☐ Add remaining chicken fat or oil and onions. Cook until onion is softened and beginning to color, 3 to 5 minutes. Stir in garlic and cook 1 minute longer. Pour in tomatoes and their juice, stirring to break up tomatoes and scrape up any meat juices. Add mango purée, salt, red-pepper flakes, chili powder, cinnamon stick, bay leaves and honey and cook, stirring often, 2 to 3 minutes.

☐ Return beef to Dutch oven and pour in enough water to just cover meat. Cover tightly and simmer, over medium-low heat, 1½ hours. (Check from time to time to see if there is enough water.) Add carrots, sweet potato chunks, prunes and beans. Cover and cook, over medium heat, 30 minutes longer adding a little more water if necessary.

☐ Remove meat to a deep serving platter. If liquid is too thin, reduce over medium-high heat until slightly thickened, 5 to 10 minutes. Spoon vegetables and beans around beef. Pour sauce over meat and sprinkle meat and vegetables with chopped coriander. Serve meat cut into thin slices.

ABOVE COLORFUL DECORATION ON BOATS IN THE HODEIDAH FISH MARKET IN YEMEN.

HAMIN

8 SERVINGS

Hamin, from the Hebrew for cholent, is the Sephardic version of the same slowly cooked stew. The Iranians, Afghanis and Kurds use quinces and flower-scented waters, especially rosewater, in their cooking, and this recipe uses both. Originally dried rose buds or rose petals were used, but rosewater is more easily available at Greek and Middle Eastern grocery stores. These flavors provide a more exotic and highly perfumed dish which can be made with chicken, beef or, as used in this recipe, lamb.

- 2 tablespoons vegetable oil
- 2 onions, thinly sliced
- 4 garlic cloves, finely chopped
- 5 to 6 pounds shoulder of lamb, boned, trimmed of fat and cut into large cubes
- 4 potatoes, peeled and sliced
- 4 carrots, thinly sliced
- 1 pound pumpkin or butternut squash, peeled and cut into cubes
- 2½ cups basmati or American long-grain rice, rinsed and drained
- 1 pound quinces, peeled, quartered, cored and sliced
- 1 cinnamon stick
- 4 whole cloves
- 2 teaspoons salt
- Freshly ground black pepper
- 1 tablespoon rosewater (optional)
- 2 eggs, lightly beaten

COOK'S TIP

AS LAMB MAY CONTAIN ADDITIONAL FAT, IT IS DESIRABLE TO PREPARE THIS 2 DAYS AHEAD. LEAVE TO COOL, THEN REFRIGERATE. WHEN COLD, SCRAPE OFF ANY CONGEALED FAT FROM SURFACE AND REHEAT IN A 350°F OVEN FOR 1 HOUR.

☐ In a large Dutch oven with tight-fitting lid, over medium-high heat, heat oil. Add onions and cook until just golden, 5 to 7 minutes. Stir in garlic and cook 1 minute longer. Remove to plate and set aside.

☐ Into same Dutch oven, add meat and cook on all sides until pieces are well browned, 7 to 10 minutes. You may need to cook in batches – do not crowd pot. Remove meat to another plate and remove Dutch oven from heat, leaving any remaining oil.

☐ Preheat oven to 450°F. Cover bottom of the Dutch oven with potato slices, spreading them evenly. Add carrots in one layer and then squash cubes. Add rice and meat. Cover meat with onion-garlic mixture, spreading to cover meat. Top with quince slices, cinnamon stick and cloves and sprinkle with salt and pepper to taste. Sprinkle with rosewater if using.

☐ Mix eggs with 1 cup water and pour into pot with enough cold water to cover the ingredients. Cook for 30 minutes, then reduce heat to lowest setting, around 200°F, and continue cooking 8 to 10 hours or overnight. Serve the hamin from Dutch oven.

ABOVE CHILDREN OFFERING THE FIRST FRUITS FOR *SHAVUOT* (FEAST OF WEEKS) ALSO KNOWN AS THE FESTIVAL OF FRUITS.

SWEET-AND-SOUR STUFFED CABBAGE

6 TO 8 SERVINGS

There are many versions of this traditional Sukkot dish in the Eastern-European Jewish tradition, with as many names. *Goluptsy*, as it is called in Russia, is made with a sweet-and-sour tomato-based sauce. In other countries, such as Hungary, it is not. This is the recipe my aunt used to prepare for my father. He loved it served with mashed potatoes.

- 1 large cabbage
- ½ cup dried seasoned bread crumbs
- ½ cup milk
- 1 tablespoon vegetable oil
- 1 onion, finely chopped
- 2 garlic cloves, peeled and finely chopped
- 2 pounds ground beef
- ¾ teaspoon salt
- Freshly ground black pepper
- ¼ cup catsup
- 2 eggs, beaten
- 2 to 3 tablespoons chopped fresh dill

- ½ cup American long-grain rice
- Chopped fresh dill for garnish

SAUCE
- 1 28-ounce can tomatoes
- 1 16-ounce can tomato sauce
- ½ cup catsup
- Salt
- Freshly ground pepper
- 2 onions, thinly sliced
- Grated zest and juice of 1 lemon
- ⅓ cup light brown sugar
- ⅔ cup golden raisins

□ Core center out of cabbage and gently remove as many leaves as possible; smaller leaves can be overlapped to form a large leaf. Bring a large saucepan of water to a boil. Plunge in leaves (it may be necessary to do this in batches) and simmer until the leaves are softened, but not cooked tender, 3–5 minutes. Drain into a colander and rinse under cold running water; set aside.

□ In a small bowl, combine bread crumbs and milk and leave to stand until milk is absorbed.

□ In a small skillet, over medium-high heat, heat oil. Add onion and cook until onion is softened and beginning to color, 3 to 5 minutes. Add garlic and cook 1 minute longer, stirring occasionally. Remove from heat and set aside.

□ In a large bowl, with a fork, mix beef, salt and pepper to taste, catsup, eggs, chopped dill and rice. Stir in milk-soaked bread crumbs and cooked onions; mix until very well blended.

□ In a shallow roasting pan with tight-fitting lid, combine all sauce ingredients. Over medium-high heat, bring to a boil, then reduce heat and simmer, stirring occasionally, 15 to 20 minutes.

□ Preheat oven to 325°F. Arrange a cabbage leaf on a flat work surface, remove any heavy core from leaf if necessary. Place 1 to 2 tablespoons meat mixture (exact amount will depend on the size of the leaf) in center of each cabbage leaf. Fold sides over stuffing, then roll cabbage leaf jelly-roll fashion to completely enclose the stuffing. Place on a cookie sheet or tray and continue until all meat mixture is used. (Any leftover cabbage can be thinly shredded and added to the sauce.)

□ Arrange all cabbage packages, seam-sides down, in the sauce-filled roasting pan and spoon some sauce over cabbage packages. Add a little water if necessary; cabbages should be *just* covered with liquid. Cover and cook about 1½ hours.

□ Remove cover and baste cabbage packages with sauce. With a slotted spoon, remove packages to a deep serving plate and keep warm. If liquid is very thin, reduce over medium-high heat until slightly thickened. If it is too thick, add a little water; pour over cabbage and sprinkle with the chopped dill.

ABOVE A POIGNANT REMINDER OF THE JEWISH COMMUNITY ON THIS HOUSE IN THE OLD QUARTER OF KRAKOW, POLAND.

OLD-FASHIONED POT ROAST WITH ONION GRAVY

8 TO 10 SERVINGS

This typical Russian-Jewish dish has become a staple of the American-Jewish repertoire. There are many versions, probably the most well-known is the shortcut recipe made with a package of onion soup mix! This is just as easy and made with the real thing; it is best served with mashed potatoes.

- 1 5- to 6-pound first-cut brisket of beef or boneless beef shoulder
- 1 tablespoon all-purpose flour
- 4 tablespoons vegetable oil
- 6 onions, cut into ½-inch rings
- 4 to 6 garlic cloves, peeled and finely chopped
- 1 cup tomato juice
- Salt
- Freshly ground black pepper
- ½ teaspoon dried thyme
- ½ teaspoon paprika
- 1 bay leaf

- 6 carrots, cut into ¼-inch slices on the diagonal
- Fresh parsley sprigs to garnish

COOK'S TIP

AS WITH ALL SLOWLY COOKED STEWS AND MEATS, THIS DISH IS BEST COOKED A DAY AHEAD. REFRIGERATE AND SKIM OFF CONGEALED FAT FROM SURFACE. REHEAT IN A 350°F OVEN FOR 35 TO 40 MINUTES.

☐ Rinse meat under cold running water; pat dry with paper towels. Trim any visible fat, then dust meat with flour.

☐ In a large Dutch oven, over medium-high heat, heat 2 tablespoons oil. Add meat and cook until browned on underside, 5 to 7 minutes. Turn meat and cook until underside is browned, 5 to 6 minutes longer. Remove to a plate.

☐ Preheat oven to 325°F. Add remaining oil to Dutch oven and stir in onions. Cook until onions begin to soften and color, 4 to 5 minutes. Add garlic and cook 1 minute longer. Pour in tomato juice, stirring and scraping to pick up any bits from bottom. Season with salt and pepper to taste, thyme, paprika and bay leaf.

☐ Return beef to pot and add enough water to cover all ingredients. Bring to a boil and skim any foam that comes to the surface. Cover tightly and cook in the oven until beef is fork-tender, 3 to 3½ hours. Add carrots to pot and cook until tender, 30 minutes longer.

☐ Remove Dutch oven from the oven and remove cover. If liquid is too thin, remove the beef to a deep serving platter and reduce gravy to thicken slightly. Spoon gravy with onions and carrots around beef and garnish with parsley. Serve meat carved into ¼-inch slices.

CHOLENT

8 TO 10 SERVINGS

Cholent is a long-simmering stew cooked on Friday night and served at noon after the Sabbath morning service. It has probably been made since Biblical times and is found in all Jewish communities, but with slightly differing ingredients and flavorings; the essential ingredients being meat and beans. The key is the long, slow cooking to tenderize an economical cut of meat and that the stew can be left to cook for a long time at a low temperature.

A cholent, meaning "hot-slow" in French, is made by every Ashkenazic Jewish family and is really a layered hotpot that can include meat, chicken, beans, sausages, dumplings and potatoes. Its counterpart is found in the Sephardic dfina, which is prepared all over the Middle East. A hamin, from the Hebrew for cholent, is eaten by Jews along the Afghan border, as well as in Iran, Italy and Israel.

This is a typical Ashkenazic version and contains a special dumpling called a cholent knaidle.

- 2 tablespoons vegetable oil
- 4 onions, cut in half and sliced
- 4 garlic cloves, peeled and finely chopped
- 3 pounds boneless flank, brisket or beef shoulder, cut into large cubes
- 2 cups dried lima, navy, great northern or red kidney beans, soaked at least 8 hours
- 1 cup pot barley
- 10 to 12 medium potatoes, peeled and halved or, if large, quartered
- 2 teaspoons salt

- Freshly ground black pepper
- 1½ teaspoons dried thyme
- 1 teaspoon paprika
- 2 bay leaves
- 2 tablespoons sugar

CHOLENT KNAIDLE
- 1½ cups all-purpose flour
- ¾ teaspoon baking powder
- ½ teaspoon salt
- Freshly ground black pepper
- ¾ cup finely chopped chicken fat, beef suet or soft margarine
- 2 tablespoons chopped fresh parsley

☐ In a large Dutch oven with tight-fitting lid, over medium-high heat, heat oil. Add onions and cook until well browned, 7 to 10 minutes. Stir in garlic and cook 1 minute longer. Remove to a plate and set aside.

☐ Into same Dutch oven, add meat and cook on all sides until pieces are well browned, 7 to 10 minutes. You may need to cook in batches – do not crowd pot. Remove meat to another plate and remove Dutch oven from heat, leaving any remaining oil.

☐ Return onions and garlic to Dutch oven, spreading them evenly over bottom. Drain beans and add them, then layer in beef cubes, barley and potatoes, sprinkling salt, pepper to

taste, thyme and paprika between layers. Tuck in bay leaves.

☐ In a small saucepan, over high heat, bring sugar to a boil with 2 tablespoons water. Cook until sugar turns a dark caramel color, 1 to 2 minutes. Off the heat and holding pan away from you, carefully pour in ¼ cup cold water (caramel will splatter). Return to heat to liquidize caramel, then pour into Dutch oven.

☐ Pour in enough water to just cover meat, vegetables and bean layers and, over high heat, bring to a boil. Skim off any foam which comes to the surface. Lower heat slightly and cook 30 minutes, skimming occasionally. Add a little more water if necessary to be sure all ingredients are covered.

☐ Prepare knaidle. Preheat oven to 200°F or lowest setting. Into a medium bowl, sift flour, baking powder, salt and pepper to taste. Cut in chicken fat, suet or margarine. Add chopped parsley and 4 to 6 tablespoons cold water, then stir to form a soft dough. Form into large dumpling or a sausage shape.

☐ Remove Dutch oven from heat. Gently place knaidle on top of ingredients in the Dutch oven, tucking it in gently. Cover tightly and cook in the very low oven 10 to 12 hours or overnight. Serve cholent from the Dutch oven; slice the knaidle into serving pieces or serve separately.

SHASHLIK

6 SERVINGS

Shashlik, shish kabob and kebab are terms which mean lamb or beef grilled on a skewer. Skewered meat cooked over an open fire was probably one of the original ways of cooking meat. Traditional in the Russian republics, the Balkans and the Middle East, its modern form, the barbecue, is very popular in Israel and the United States. Israeli street food often features skewers of marinated cubed lamb, and many Russian-Jewish immigrants now sell shashlik beside the traditional hot dog men in New York City! Serve with rice and Israeli Salad (see page 89).

MARINADE

- ¾ cup olive oil
- ½ cup lemon juice
- ½ cup dry red wine or dry sherry
- 2 to 3 tablespoons chopped fresh rosemary, or 1 tablespoon dried
- ½ small onion, finely chopped or grated
- 4 to 6 garlic cloves, peeled and finely chopped
- 1 teaspoon salt
- Freshly ground black pepper
- ½ teaspoon red-pepper flakes (optional)

- 4 pounds boneless lamb shoulder, trimmed of all visible fat and cut into 2-inch cubes
- 4 small onions, root ends attached, cut into eighths
- 1 pound cherry tomatoes
- 2 yellow or red sweet peppers, cored, seeded and cut into 1-inch squares
- Fresh rosemary sprigs for garnish

☐ In a large, shallow nonmetalic baking dish, combine marinade ingredients, stirring until well blended and creamy. Add lamb cubes and stir around until well coated. Cover and refrigerate 6 hours or overnight, stirring occasionally.

☐ Position barbecue rack about 5 inches above preheated coals.

☐ Thread lamb cubes on to metal skewers, leaving a small space between cubes so meat cooks evenly. Thread onion pieces, cherry tomatoes and pepper squares on to separate skewers; brush with some remaining marinade.

☐ Arrange lamb skewers over center of coals and cook, turning and basting with marinade occasionally, 17 to 20 minutes. Halfway through cooking time, add vegetable skewers to barbecue and cook, turning and basting with marinade, 8 to 10 minutes.

☐ Arrange skewers on long serving platter and surround with fresh sprigs of rosemary. Serve with rice, Israeli Salad or other accompaniments separately.

ABOVE IT IS CUSTOMARY FOR JEWS TO GO TO THE WESTERN WALL
IN JERUSALEM TO PRAY ON THE SABBATH.

✡

STUFFED PASSOVER LAMB

6 TO 8 SERVINGS

Although some Jewish communities do not eat lamb at Passover, it is traditional throughout the Middle East and other lamb-producing countries, such as England. It is a popular choice for a Sephardic Passover Seder because young lamb is at its best in springtime. As with other meats, the hindquarters are not generally kosher, so the shoulder is preferable. Ask your butcher to bone the lamb and cut a pocket for the stuffing.

STUFFING

- 1 tablespoon olive or vegetable oil
- 1 onion, finely chopped
- 2 garlic cloves, peeled and finely chopped
- ½ pound lean ground lamb
- ½ cup American long-grain rice
- Salt
- Freshly ground black pepper
- ½ teaspoon ground cumin
- ⅛ teaspoon turmeric
- 1 tablespoon chopped fresh coriander
- ½ cup chopped walnuts or almonds
- ½ cup raisins
- ½ cup chopped dried apricots
- 1 egg, beaten
- 1 4- to 5-pound shoulder of lamb, boned, pocketed and well trimmed of fat
- 2 tablespoons olive oil
- 2 tablespoons honey
- 2 tablespoons potatostarch
- 1 cup beef or chicken stock
- 1 tablespoon cider vinegar
- Fresh watercress for garnish

☐ Prepare stuffing. In a medium skillet over medium-high heat, heat oil. Add onion and cook until onion begins to soften and color, 3 to 5 minutes. Stir in garlic and cook 1 minute longer.

☐ Add ground lamb and cook, stirring with a fork to break up meat, until meat is no longer pink, 4 to 5 minutes. Stir in rice and cook until rice turns golden and translucent, 5 minutes longer. Pour in ⅓ cup hot water, salt and pepper to taste, cumin and turmeric. Cook, covered, over medium-low heat, until rice is just tender and all liquid has been absorbed, 12 to 15 minutes. Remove from heat and cool slightly. Stir in coriander, nuts, raisins, apricots and beaten egg.

☐ Preheat oven to 350°F. Lay meat on work surface, skin side down. Season with salt and pepper to taste and spread stuffing evenly over the meat to within 1 inch of edges. Roll up meat as neatly as possible and tie at 2-inch intervals with kitchen string. Rub surface of meat with olive oil and sprinkle with salt and pepper.

☐ Place meat, seam-side down, on a rack in a roasting pan. Roast for 20 minutes per pound for medium. About 20 minutes before meat is done, brush with the honey. Return to oven.

☐ Remove lamb to a serving platter, cover with foil, keep warm and leave to stand 15 minutes.

☐ Meanwhile, remove rack from pan and pour off all but about 2 tablespoons fat. Mix potatostarch with ¼ cup water and pour into pan with stock and vinegar. Bring to a boil, stirring often, and reduce heat to medium-low and simmer until smooth and slightly thickened, 7 to 10 minutes.

☐ Pour gravy into gravy boat to serve separately. Garnish lamb with watercress.

ABOVE NOTE THE *PEYOT* (SIDELOCKS) ON THESE TWO SEPHARDIC JEWS.

FISH DISHES

Gefilte Fish

Curried Fish Fillets

Baked Salmon with Avocado-Dill Sauce

Jewish-Style Fried Fish

Red Snapper with Green Sauce

Baked Trout with Pomegranate

Sweet-and-Sour Fish

GEFILTE FISH

6 SERVINGS

The title gefilte fish comes from the German for "filled fish." Originally, skinned and boned fish was stuffed with a minced fish mixture and slowly simmered. After chilling, the rich stock became jellied and was served as part of the dish or separately. Nowadays, however, the mixture is generally formed into balls and simmered in stock. It is also very attractive when packed into a ring mold and baked in the oven, or even microwaved! Of course, cooked in this way there is no jelly as an accompaniment.

Although freshwater carp and pike were traditional for making gefilte fish, most cooks prefer a mixture of saltwater white fish. But whatever fish you use, gefilte fish is always served with carrot slices and beet-flavored horseradish sauce!

FISH STOCK
- 3- to 4-pounds fish bones and heads (white fish only), well rinsed
- 2 onions, sliced
- 1 carrot, sliced
- 1 stalk celery, sliced
- 1 leek, split lengthwise, sliced and well rinsed
- 4 sprigs fresh parsley
- 1 teaspoon salt
- 1 teaspoon black peppercorns
- 2 sprigs fresh thyme (optional)

FISH MIXTURE
- 3 pounds white fish fillets, such as cod, whiting, snapper, grouper (a little carp or pike can be mixed in)
- 2 onions, quartered
- Salt
- 3 eggs, lightly beaten
- ½ teaspoon fresh ground white pepper
- ¼ teaspoon grated nutmeg (optional)
- ½ cup medium matzo meal
- 1 carrot, thinly sliced
- Fresh parsley sprigs and lemon slices to garnish
- Horseradish-Beet Sauce (see page 15), or bottled, for serving

☐ Prepare stock. Into a large stockpot, place all ingredients for fish stock. Cover with cold water and, over high heat, bring to a boil. Skim off any foam that comes to the surface. Reduce heat and simmer for 20 minutes. Strain stock into a large saucepot or Dutch oven. Set aside.

☐ Prepare fish mixture. Into a food processor fitted with metal blade, place fish and onions and process to a fine purée. (You may need to work in batches.) Add 1½ teaspoons salt, or to taste, eggs, pepper and nutmeg and process to mix.

☐ Stir in matzo meal; add ¼ cup water, a little at a time. The mixture should be light and slightly sticky, but hold its shape. Cover and refrigerate for 30 minutes.

☐ Using 2 tablespoons, form mixture into ovals, placing each on a cookie sheet sprinkled with water. Continue until all mixture is shaped.

☐ Bring stock to a boil. Add carrot slices and carefully drop fish ovals into stock. Reduce heat and simmer gently for 1 hour. (Do not leave water to boil.)

☐ Leave fish to cool in stock. Using a slotted spoon, remove fish ovals to a large shallow baking dish or serving platter. Strain stock over the fish ovals and place a carrot slice on top of each oval; scatter remaining slices around the dish. Refrigerate 4 hours or overnight. Garnish with parsley sprigs and lemon slices and serve with Horseradish-Beet Sauce.

CURRIED FISH FILLETS

6 SERVINGS

This dish comes from one of the Jewish communities in India, the southern city of Cochin. Cochin is near the Kerala Coast which produces fresh fish and is also famous for its spice market. This is best served with rice.

- 1 tablespoon vegetable oil
- 1 onion, cut in half and thinly sliced
- 2 to 3 garlic cloves, peeled and finely chopped
- 2 pounds white fish fillets, such as flounder, cod, halibut or whiting, cut in 3-inch pieces
- 1 cup chopped fresh coriander leaves
- 1 tablespoon white- or red-wine vinegar
- ¼ cup tomato paste
- 1 teaspoon ground cumin
- ½ teaspoon turmeric
- 1 small fresh red chili, or ½ teaspoon red-pepper flakes
- Fresh coriander sprigs for garnish
- Hot boiled rice for serving

☐ In a large skillet, over medium-high heat, heat oil. Add sliced onion and cook until softened and beginning to color, 3 to 5 minutes. Add garlic and cook 1 minute longer.

☐ Add fish and cook until the fish begins to firm and turn opaque, 4 to 5 minutes. Gently stir in remaining ingredients, except garnish and rice, and ½ cup water and simmer 15 minutes, covered. The fish will flake easily if tested with the tip of a knife.

☐ Remove fish fillets to a serving dish. Increase heat to high and cook sauce until slightly thickened, 2 to 3 minutes. Pour over fish fillets. Garnish with coriander sprigs and serve with hot rice.

BAKED SALMON WITH AVOCADO-DILL SAUCE

12 TO 14 SERVINGS

A whole fish baked in foil makes an ideal party or holiday dish. It can be served hot or cold and is kosher for Passover. Poaching a fish requires a large fish kettle or poacher, but baking it gives excellent results as well. If the fish is too big to fit on a cookie sheet, cut it in half, then reassemble it for serving. Fish seems tastiest served at room temperature; just as well, as this provides time for adding festive garnishes and preparing sauces and accompaniments.

- 1 5- to 6-pound whole salmon or sea trout, dressed with head and tail
- Salt
- 1 lemon, sliced
- 4 to 5 scallions, cut in half lengthwise
- 3 to 4 fresh parsley sprigs
- 3 to 4 fresh dill sprigs
- Vegetable oil
- Thin slices of cucumber (optional)
- Salad leaves, fresh dill sprigs, and lemon slices for garnish

AVOCADO-DILL SAUCE
- 1 large avocado
- 6 sprigs fresh dill
- ½ teaspoon salt
- 4 egg yolks
- Freshly ground black pepper
- ¼ cup lemon juice or cider vinegar, or half and half
- ½ cup (1 stick) unsalted butter or soft margarine
- Cayenne pepper

☐ Preheat oven to 350°F. Wash fish well, inside and out, under cold running water; do not dry. Sprinkle cavity with salt and stuff with lemon slices, scallions, parsley and dill.

☐ Lightly grease a wide piece of foil long enough to enclose fish. Center foil lengthwise on a large cookie sheet and place fish in center. Bring 2 long ends up over fish and fold together stopping a few inches from fish; bring together and fold up short sides of foil, forming a large envelope around fish with lots of room for expansion.

☐ Bake fish in foil for 1 hour. Leave fish to cool slightly, about 15 minutes, before unwrapping. Carefully fold back foil, reserve juices if using for a sauce, or discard.

☐ Using a long thin knife, cut along length of backbone. Beginning behind head, peel off skin, pulling out fins as you go, until you reach tail. Scrape off thin layer of brown flesh which runs down the center of fish.

☐ Carefully center serving platter over skinned fish and, holding fish on cookie sheet against serving platter, flip them over so skinned side of fish is against serving plate. Remove skin and brown flesh from top side. Clean edges of plate.

☐ To serve, arrange salad leaves around fish and garnish fish with thin slices of cucumber, overlapping to imitate scales or garnish with dill sprigs and lemon slices. Cover loosely and refrigerate until ready to serve. Accompany with Avocado-Dill Sauce.

☐ Make sauce. Cut avocado in half, remove pit and peel off skin. In a food processor fitted with metal blade, process avocado flesh until smooth. Scrape into a mixing bowl and scrape processor clean.

☐ Into processor, place dill, salt and egg yolks and process until dill is finely chopped; season with pepper to taste.

☐ In a small saucepan, over high heat, bring lemon juice or vinegar to a boil. With processor running, slowly pour boiling liquid over yolk mixture and process 1 minute.

☐ In same saucepan, over medium-high heat, bring butter or margarine to a boil. With processor running, slowly pour in hot butter or margarine. Stop processor, add avocado purée and a pinch of cayenne pepper and process 1 minute longer or until well blended and smooth. Taste for seasoning and pour into serving bowl. Refrigerate until ready to serve.

COOK'S TIP

FISH IS BEST SERVED COOL OR AT ROOM TEMPERATURE. IF PREPARING AHEAD, REMOVE FISH FROM REFRIGERATOR 2 TO 3 HOURS BEFORE SERVING.

JEWISH-STYLE FRIED FISH

6 SERVINGS

Introduced by Sephardic Jews in the 1600s, fried fish is now a favorite Friday night supper among many Jewish communities. Somehow it tastes better cold than hot, so it is an ideal choice for a Sabbath supper, as it can be prepared early in the day. Be sure to fry in oil, not butter, and keep in a cool place, not the refrigerator if possible, as the fish will stay crisper much longer. A mixture of half medium and half fine matzo meal is best for the coating.

- 3 pounds fish fillets or steaks, such as flounder, halibut, salmon, herring, or any combination
- Salt
- ¾ cup all-purpose flour
- ¼ teaspoon freshly ground black pepper
- 2 eggs, beaten
- 1 cup matzo meal
- Vegetable oil for frying
- Lemon wedges and parsley sprigs for garnish

☐ Rinse fish fillets or steaks in cold water and sprinkle lightly with salt. Place in a colander and leave to drain for 30 minutes. Pat dry with paper towels.

☐ Into 3 pie plates or shallow dishes, place flour, beaten eggs, seasoned with black pepper, and matzo meal. Dip each piece of fish first into flour, shaking off any excess; then into the egg and brush to coat evenly, finally into matzo meal. Be sure the fish is completely coated with meal to prevent any moisture escaping during frying.

☐ In a deep-fat fryer or large skillet, over medium-high heat, heat about ½ inch vegetable oil to 350°F. Add several pieces of fish and fry until underside is well browned, 4 to 5 minutes. Using a metal pancake turner, gently turn fish and fry until other side is brown, 3 to 4 minutes. Remove to paper towels to drain.

☐ Continue frying in batches until all fish is fried, adding more oil as necessary. (Do not try to fry too many pieces at a time or the temperature of the oil will fall too low and the fish will "stew" rather than fry.)

☐ Arrange fish on a serving dish and store in a cool place, loosely covered. Serve with lemon wedges and parsley sprigs. (Fish can be served hot; keep pieces warm in a 350°F oven until all fish is cooked, then serve at once.)

RED SNAPPER WITH GREEN SAUCE

6 SERVINGS

When I spent a summer in Mexico with a Jewish-Mexican family many years ago, they baked fish or chicken in a vegetable and herb purée "blanket", which kept the flesh moist and tender. This was made by hand in a mortar and pestle, but the food processor now makes this work easy.

- Vegetable oil for greasing
- 3 to 4 pounds red snapper or sea bass fillets
- Fresh juice of 5 limes
- Salt
- Freshly ground black pepper
- Cherry tomatoes, ripe olives and chopped fresh coriander leaves for garnish

SAUCE
- 1 head romaine lettuce, trimmed, cored and shredded
- ½ cucumber, peeled and seeded
- 1 small green pepper, cored, seeded and chopped
- 1 red onion, quartered
- 3 to 4 garlic cloves
- 1 small bunch watercress, stems trimmed
- 4 to 5 scallions, trimmed
- ½ cup coriander leaves

☐ Lightly grease a deep baking dish. Place fish in center of dish and rub with a little lime juice. Sprinkle with salt and pepper to taste. Set aside.

☐ Make the sauce. In a food processor fitted with metal blade, process lettuce, cucumber, green pepper, red onion, garlic, watercress, scallions and coriander leaves with remaining lime juice. Pour sauce over fish, cover and refrigerate at least 2 hours.

☐ Preheat oven to 350°F. Uncover fish and bake, basting twice, until fish is opaque and flesh flakes when pierced with a knife, 20 to 25 minutes. Remove fish to serving platter. Pour sauce over and garnish with cherry tomatoes, ripe olives and coriander leaves.

BAKED TROUT WITH POMEGRANATE

4 SERVINGS

This dish is typical of the kind of "New Wave" Jewish cooking happening in Israel today. Trout farms have been introduced to the Galilee region, and this classic Western fish has now become very popular. Pomegranates are one of the many exotic fruits widely available in the Middle East and historically important in Jewish cooking.

- 1 large ripe pomegranate
- 1 tablespoon olive oil
- 1 onion, finely chopped
- 2 garlic cloves, peeled and finely chopped
- 1 cup coarsely chopped pecans
- 4 tablespoons chopped fresh parsley
- Salt
- Freshly ground black pepper
- ¼ teaspoon ground cardamom
- 2 tablespoons wine vinegar
- 4 tablespoons butter or margarine, melted
- 4 trout, 10 to 12-ounces each, cleaned and dressed
- Curly kale for garnish

☐ With a sharp knife, cut top off pomegranate. Score fruit in about 6 wedges and pull apart into separate sections. Gently scoop seeds into a small bowl. Set aside.

☐ In a medium skillet, over medium-high heat, heat olive oil. Add onion and cook until softened and beginning to color, 3 to 5 minutes. Add garlic and cook 1 minute longer.

☐ Stir in pecans, parsley, salt and black pepper to taste, cardamom, vinegar and half melted butter or margarine. Remove from heat. Stir in three-quarters of the pomegranate seeds.

☐ Preheat oven to 400°F. Lightly grease a large shallow baking dish. Rinse fish under cold running water and pat dry with paper towels. Score each fish in 2 places on each side. Spoon one-quarter of the onion mixture into each fish.

☐ Arrange fish in baking dish, drizzle with remaining butter or margarine and bake, uncovered, until flesh flakes easily if tested with tip of a knife, 12 to 15 minutes. Serve fish on a bed of curly kale and sprinkle with remaining pomegranate seeds.

SWEET-AND-SOUR FISH

6 SERVINGS

In Eastern Europe, sweet-and-sour fish was generally prepared with carp. In France it is known as *carpe à la Juive* (Jewish-style carp) and it was traditional to serve the head of the fish to the head of the house on the Jewish New Year, Rosh Hashana. This recipe uses fish steaks rather than a whole fish.

- 6 fish steaks, such as carp, pike, salmon or trout, 1 inch thick (3 pounds total weight)
- Salt
- Freshly ground black pepper
- 1 onion, thinly sliced
- 1 carrot, thinly sliced
- 1 bay leaf
- 4 to 6 whole cloves
- 1 lemon, sliced and seeds removed
- 2 to 4 slices fresh ginger root
- 1 tablespoon black peppercorns
- ½ cup red-wine vinegar
- ½ cup light brown sugar
- ½ cup seedless raisins
- 4 gingersnaps, crushed to crumbs (optional)
- 3 to 4 tablespoons, chopped fresh parsley
- Lemon twists for garnish

☐ Rinse fish steaks under cold running water and pat dry with paper towels. Sprinkle lightly with salt and pepper to taste and set aside.

☐ In a large, nonaluminum deep skillet combine onion, carrot, bay leaf, cloves, lemon slices, ginger root and peppercorns with 1 quart cold water. Over high heat, bring to a boil, then simmer, covered, for 15 minutes.

☐ Add fish steaks and cook over medium-low heat, covered, until fish pulls away from center bone and turns opaque, 10 to 12 minutes. Using a metal pancake turner, carefully remove fish steaks to a large deep glass or ceramic baking dish.

☐ Bring cooking liquid to a boil again and cook until liquid is reduced by half, 7 to 10 minutes. Strain into a smaller saucepan and add the vinegar, brown sugar and raisins. Simmer 2 to 3 minutes longer, stir in the gingersnap crumbs, if using, and chopped parsley. Cool slightly, then pour over fish. Cool completely, then refrigerate overnight. Serve chilled garnished with lemon twists.

ABOVE SUCCULENT FISH PULLED FROM THE BOUNTIFUL WATERS OF THE TURKISH COAST.

Accompaniments

Leek Fritters

Latkes

New Year Carrot Tzimmes Loaf

Sweet-and-Sour Red Cabbage

Spicy Indian-Style Potatoes

Homemade Noodles

Savory Noodle Kugel

Sweet Potato and Parsnip Kugel

Kreplach

Kasha Varnishkes

Fidellos Tostados

Indian Rice with Tomatoes and Spinach

Romanian-Style Mamaliga

Chelou

Quick-and-Easy Couscous

LEEK FRITTERS

4 SERVINGS

Leeks are an ancient vegetable, frequently used in the Sephardic Jewish kitchens. These leek patties are eaten at Passover by Greek Jews. They make a delicious vegetable accompaniment to roast poultry and meat dishes. A more hearty version made with ground meat is served as a main course.

- 2 pounds leeks, split in half lengthwise and well rinsed
- 2 eggs, beaten
- At least ¼ cup fine matzo meal (cake meal)
- Salt
- Freshly ground black pepper
- ½ teaspoon dried thyme
- ¼ teaspoon ground cinnamon
- Vegetable oil for frying
- Lemon wedges for serving

☐ In a large skillet half filled with water, over high heat, boil leeks until just tender, 5 to 7 minutes. Drain under cold running water.

☐ On a cutting board, chop leeks finely. Squeeze in a clean dish towel to remove any excess liquid. Remove to a large bowl.

☐ Stir in beaten eggs, matzo meal, salt and pepper to taste, thyme and cinnamon until well blended. Batter should be soft enough to drop by spoonfuls; add a little more matzo meal or water if necessary.

☐ In a large deep skillet, over medium-high heat, heat about 1-inch oil or enough to just cover fritters. Drop batter by tablespoonsful into the hot oil and cook until underside is browned, 2 minutes. Turn and cook until second side is browned, 1 minute longer.

☐ Remove to a serving platter and keep warm in a 300°F oven. Continue until all batter is used, adding a little more oil if necessary. Serve immediately garnished with lemon wedges.

LATKES

6 TO 8 SERVINGS

Latkes are a well-known and well-loved vegetable dish in the Jewish repertoire. Cooked in oil, these potato pancakes are traditional at Hanukah because they symbolize the miracle of the oil which lasted eight days. They are delicious with rich roast poultry, such as duck and goose, but can also be eaten as a brunch dish or on their own sprinkled with sugar or topped with applesauce or sour cream. Even before the days of the food processor, my mother's were the best.

- 6 medium potatoes, peeled
- 1 onion
- 2 eggs, lightly beaten
- ½ cup fine matzo meal, or all-purpose flour
- 1 teaspoon salt
- Pinch ground white pepper
- Vegetable oil for frying
- Applesauce or sour cream for serving

☐ In a food processor fitted with grater attachment, grate potatoes and onion. Drain in a colander, pressing to squeeze out as much liquid as possible. Place in a large bowl and beat in remaining ingredients except oil and accompaniments. (Work as quickly as possible so potatoes do not turn brown.)

☐ In a large heavy skillet, over medium-high heat, heat about 1-inch vegetable oil or just enough to cover pancakes. Drop batter by tablespoonful into hot oil and cook until underside is browned, 2 minutes. Turn and cook until second side is browned, 1 to 2 minutes longer.

☐ Remove to a serving platter and keep warm in a 300°F oven. Continue until all batter is used, adding a little more oil if necessary. Serve immediately with applesauce or sour cream.

NEW YEAR CARROT TZIMMES LOAF

8 TO 10 SERVINGS

Carrots symbolize prosperity and hope because of their rich golden color, so they are served at the New Year, Rosh Hashana. They are often the base of a meatless tzimmes, a composite stew, or bake. In Yiddish, a tzimmes means a mess or a fuss; to make a tzimmes over someone or something means to make a great fuss — usually the grandmothers' province.
This recipe is particularly fussy, but is well worth the effort and can be prepared ahead. Using traditional ingredients, I based this version on an appetizer I used to prepare at the Quai d'Orsay restaurant in Paris, Chef Antoine Bouterin's individual carrot "pâtés" made with carrots and blanched artichokes and served with a butter sauce. This is an ideal recipe for a big holiday dinner.

- 2 leeks, cut in half lengthwise and well rinsed
- 2 large carrots, cooked and mashed
- 1 large sweet potato, cooked and mashed
- 2 tablespoons pareve margarine, melted, or vegetable oil
- 2 tablespoons honey
- 1 tablespoon lemon juice
- Salt
- Freshly ground black pepper
- ¼ teaspoon cayenne pepper, or to taste
- ¼ teaspoon grated nutmeg
- 4 scallions, finely chopped
- 4 eggs
- 2 egg yolks
- 2 large potatoes, cooked and mashed
- 2 cups pitted prunes, soaked in hot water 10 to 15 minutes
- Fresh parsley sprigs and lemon twists for garnish

☐ Fill a large saucepan with water and, over high heat, bring to a boil. Add leeks and cook until slightly softened and the color brightens, 1 to 2 minutes. Drain and rinse under cold running water to stop the cooking and keep color. Separate and remove to a clean dish towel and drain and dry well. Set aside.

☐ In a large bowl, combine mashed carrots and sweet potato with melted margarine or oil, honey, lemon juice, salt and pepper to taste, cayenne pepper, nutmeg and half the chopped scallions. Set aside.

☐ In a small bowl, beat 2 of the eggs and 1 yolk. Stir into carrot-sweet potato mixture. Set aside.

☐ In another bowl, place mashed potatoes. Season with salt and pepper and add the remaining scallions. In another small bowl, beat remaining 2 eggs and 1 yolk. Add to potato-scallion mixture, beating until well blended.

☐ Preheat oven to 375°F. Lightly grease a 9- × 5- × 3-inch loaf pan or long terrine dish. Lay blanched leeks across pan or dish, overlapping each slice and alternating tops and bottoms, so pan or dish is lined with white and green parts. Leave leek slices to hang over sides of pan or dish.

☐ Drain pitted prunes and pat dry with paper towels. Carefully spoon in half of the carrot-sweet potato mixture, smoothing to make an even bottom layer. Place one-third of the prunes on to carrot layer, leaving space between prunes. Cover with half the potato-scallion mixture, smoothing top to make an even layer. Sprinkle in another third of the prunes. Repeat layers with the remaining carrot-sweet potato mixture, prunes and potato-scallion mixture.

☐ Fold over ends of leeks to cover top of pan or dish and cover tightly with foil.

☐ Place pan or dish in a shallow roasting pan or baking dish. Fill the roasting pan with boiling water to about 1½ inches up side of loaf pan or terrine. Bake 1¼ hours, until knife inserted in center comes out clean, adding water to water bath if necessary. Cool tzimmes loaf completely in water bath.

☐ Remove loaf pan or dish from water bath and dry bottom of pan. Place on a dish and weight the top overnight.

☐ To serve, unmold and slice into thin slices. Run a sharp knife around edges of pan, shake gently to unmold onto serving plate. Serve chilled, the slices garnished with parsley sprigs and lemon twists.

> **COOK'S TIP**
>
> TO WEIGHT LOAF, CUT A THIN PIECE OF CARDBOARD THE SIZE OF TOP OF LOAF. WRAP WITH FOIL AND PRESS AGAINST SURFACE OF THE LOAF. PLACE 2 HEAVY CANS ON TOP OF BOARD; REFRIGERATE OVERNIGHT. TO SLICE LOAF, USE A SHARP THIN-BLADED KNIFE. RUN UNDER HOT WATER AND WIPE DRY BEFORE CUTTING EACH SLICE.

SWEET-AND-SOUR RED CABBAGE

6 TO 8 SERVINGS

Cabbage is an important ingredient in the Jewish kitchen, especially among Russian and Central European Jews, who, unfortunately, mostly overcooked it. This braised cabbage dish is especially delicious with rich meats, such as goose, duck and pot roasts. Made with green cabbage, I serve it with turkey and it is always popular.

- 2 tablespoons vegetable oil
- 1 onion, cut in half and thinly sliced
- 2 dessert apples, peeled, cored and thinly sliced
- 1 red cabbage, about 1½ pounds, quartered, cored and shredded
- ¼ cup red-wine vinegar
- 2 to 3 tablespoons light brown sugar
- ⅓ cup golden raisins (optional)
- ½ cup vegetable stock or water
- Salt
- Freshly ground black pepper

☐ In a large, heavy-bottomed, nonaluminum pan, over medium-high heat, heat oil. Add onion and cook until soft and golden, 5 to 7 minutes. Add sliced apples and cook until beginning to brown, 2 to 3 minutes.

☐ Add cabbage and remaining ingredients. Simmer, covered, stirring occasionally and adding water if necessary until cabbage is tender, 30 to 40 minutes. Uncover and cook until liquid is absorbed. Spoon into serving bowl.

COOK'S TIP

SWEET-AND-SOUR CABBAGE IS ALSO
DELICIOUS SERVED COLD. IF YOU WANT
TO MAKE THE GREEN CABBAGE VERSION,
USE WHITE-WINE VINEGAR OR LEMON
JUICE AND WHITE SUGAR.

SPICY INDIAN-STYLE POTATOES

6 TO 8 SERVINGS

This is a typical dish made by the Bene Israel Jews, who live in Bombay. I like the addition of green peas for color.

- 3 pounds waxy new or red potatoes, unpeeled and chopped
- 5 to 6 tablespoons vegetable oil
- Salt
- ½ teaspoon turmeric
- ½ teaspoon ground cumin
- ½ teaspoon chili powder
- ½ teaspoon red-pepper flakes, or ¼ teaspoon cayenne pepper

- ½ teaspoon curry powder or garam masala
- 2 teaspoons lemon juice
- 1 cup green peas (optional)
- Fresh coriander leaves for garnish (optional)

☐ Into a large saucepot, place potatoes. Cover with cold water and, over high heat, bring to a boil. Simmer until just tender, about 20 minutes; do not overcook. Drain potatoes and rinse under cold running water to cool slightly.

☐ Peel potatoes and cut into 1-inch cubes. In a large skillet, over medium-high heat, heat 4 tablespoons oil. Add salt to taste, turmeric, cumin, chili powder, red-pepper flakes or cayenne and curry powder or garam masala; stir until well blended.

☐ Add potato cubes and stir to coat with spice mixture, adding a little more oil if necessary. Add lemon juice and ¼ cup water. Cook, covered, 5 minutes.

☐ Uncover and stir in the peas, if using. Cook 2 to 3 minutes longer until peas heat through. Serve garnished with coriander leaves if wished.

HOMEMADE NOODLES

4 TO 6 SERVINGS

Pasta in some form or other is well loved throughout the Jewish world. Lokshen, Yiddish for noodles, are used by Eastern European Jews as an accompaniment to meats, stews, in soups or in puddings called kugels, egg-enriched dishes of baked noodles with sweet or savory additions. Italian Jews have pasta as a national dish, Greek and Turkish Jews use macaroni in baked meat dishes and the Middle Eastern and Sephardic Jews use thin noodles or vermicelli called fidellos. This homemade pasta can be cut into soup noodles or any other shape you like. The food processor makes this easy work.

VARIATIONS

NOODLE SQUARES (PLAETSCHEN)

PREPARE DOUGH AS ABOVE, BUT DO NOT CUT INTO NOODLES. CUT THE DOUGH SQUARES INTO ½-INCH STRIPS, THEN CUT STRIPS INTO ½-INCH PIECES, TO FORM ½-INCH SQUARES. BOIL AS ABOVE, USE IN SOUP.

BOW TIES (SHPAERTZLEN)

ROLL OUT DOUGH AS DIRECTED BUT DO NOT LEAVE TO DRY. CUT DOUGH INTO 1-INCH STRIPS, THEN CUT STRIPS INTO 1-INCH PIECES TO FORM 1-INCH SQUARES. PINCH SQUARES IN CENTER TO FORM BOW TIES. BOIL AS ABOVE; USE IN SOUPS AND WITH STEWS.

THIMBLE NOODLES (FINGERHEUTCHEN)

PREPARE DOUGH AS ABOVE, BUT DRY ONLY 15 MINUTES. FOLD DOUGH SHEET IN HALF LENGTHWISE AND, WITH A FLOURED THIMBLE OR TINY ROUND CUTTER, CUT THROUGH THE DOUBLE LAYER OF PASTA. FRY PASTA CIRCLES IN OIL HEATED TO 375°F UNTIL GOLDEN BROWN AND SLIGHTLY PUFFED. DRAIN ON PAPER TOWELS, THEN SERVE IN CHICKEN SOUP.

- 2 cups all-purpose flour
- 2 eggs
- ½ teaspoon salt

☐ In a food processor fitted with metal blade, process flour, eggs and salt until blended. With machine running, add 1 to 2 tablespoons water until dough forms a ball in the machine. (If dough is too sticky, add a little more flour.) Process 30 seconds.

☐ Turn out dough on to a lightly floured surface and knead lightly until dough is smooth and elastic. Cover dough on surface with inverted bowl and leave to rest 30 minutes.

☐ Flour 2 large cookie sheets. Cut dough in half and work with one half at a time. On lightly floured surface, roll dough as thin as possible into a 14-inch square. Place dough square on floured cookie sheet and sprinkle with flour; leave to dry 25 to 30 minutes. Repeat with second half of dough.

☐ When dough is slightly dry, fold each square sheet of pasta into a loose, flat jelly-roll shape. Slice crosswise into noodles ⅛ to ½ inch wide, depending on width you want.

☐ Unroll noodles and shake to separate, letting them stand 1 minute longer. (For later use, hang noodles over the back of a chair or wooden rack to dry.)

☐ Bring a large saucepan or kettle of water to a boil. Add noodles and cook about 5 minutes for wide noodles and 2 to 3 minutes for thin noodles. Drain and add to boiling chicken soup or toss with butter and cheese and serve immediately.

SAVORY NOODLE KUGEL

A kugel is a baked pudding popular with Eastern European Jews. Traditionally, a kugel was simmered in a separate dish, inside or alongside a cholent (see page 59) and then served as an accompaniment or afterwards with pickles. Noodle kugels can be made with sugar and fresh or dried fruits to be served as a dessert. Cheese-based kugels can be served as an accompaniment dish or a main dish dairy meal for Shavuot.

☐ Preheat oven to 350°F. Lightly grease a deep baking dish. In a large bowl, cream butter and cream cheese together until smooth and well blended. Beat in cottage or pot cheese and eggs, then slowly beat in the milk.

☐ Stir in lemon zest and juice, scallions, raisins, if using, salt and pepper to taste and nutmeg. Add noodles and toss to mix well.

☐ Turn into baking dish and cook until mixture is set and top is puffy and golden brown, 1 hour. Serve hot or cold from dish.

- ½ cup (1 stick) unsalted butter or pareve margarine, at room temperature
- ½ pound cream cheese, at room temperature
- 1 cup cottage cheese or pot cheese
- 5 eggs, beaten
- 2 cups milk
- Grated zest and juice of 1 lemon
- 2 scallions, finely chopped
- ¼ cup raisins (optional)
- Salt
- Freshly ground black pepper
- ¼ teaspoon grated nutmeg
- ½ pound broad or fine egg noodles, cooked and drained

VARIATION

BAKE KUGEL IN A WELL-GREASED RING MOLD. COOK 45 TO 50 MINUTES AND UNMOLD ON TO SERVING PLATTER. CUT IN WEDGES TO SERVE.

SWEET POTATO AND PARSNIP KUGEL

6 TO 8 SERVINGS

- 2 sweet potatoes, peeled
- 2 carrots, peeled
- 2 parsnips, peeled
- 1 apple, peeled, cored and quartered
- 1 onion, quartered
- ¼ cup (½ stick) butter, margarine or pareve margarine
- Salt
- Freshly ground black pepper
- 1 teaspoon ground cinnamon
- ½ teaspoon grated nutmeg
- ¼ cup light brown sugar
- ¼ cup light molasses or corn syrup
- 2 eggs, beaten
- ¼ cup fine matzo meal (cake meal)
- ¼ cup vegetable oil

☐ In a food processor fitted with grater attachment, grate potatoes, carrots, parsnips and apple. Scrape into large bowl and set aside. Wipe processor clean. Grate onion.

☐ Preheat oven to 375°F. In a large deep skillet, over medium-high heat, melt butter or margarine. Add onion and cook until beginning to soften, 2 to 3 minutes. Stir in grated vegetables and apple and cook just until vegetables begin to soften, 4 to 5 minutes. Scrape into large bowl.

☐ Add salt and pepper to taste, cinnamon, nutmeg, brown sugar, molasses or corn syrup and ¼ cup water. Stir well and leave to cool slightly. Add beaten eggs and matzo meal.

☐ In a medium roasting pan or 9- × 13-inch baking pan, heat vegetable oil. When a small amount of vegetable mixture sizzles when added to the oil, turn vegetable mixture into the baking pan, smoothing the top evenly. Bake, covered with foil, 30 minutes. Uncover and bake until vegetables feel soft when pierced with a knife and top is brown, 15 to 20 minutes longer.

The kugel must be one of the greatest contributions of Jewish cooking to the world. It is a baked pudding which can be savory or sweet, and, depending on the ingredients, eaten as a vegetable or dessert.
Sweet potatoes, carrots and parsnips are all naturally sweet vegetables. They combine to make a baked vegetable pudding which is particularly delicious with roast turkey and duck.

KREPLACH

ABOUT 75 PIECES

Yiddish for "little crêpe," kreplach were originally from Russia and Poland. These are small filled dumplings, sometimes referred to as Jewish ravioli or Jewish wontons. They can be made in various shapes and filled with meat, chicken, or cheese when used at Shavuot. The meat filling is usually made from the shin of beef which has been used to make the stock for the soup on Purim or before the Yom Kippur fast, but ground beef can be used instead.

- ½ pound (about 2 cups) cooked beef, ground, or ½ pound ground beef, browned
- 1 small onion, chopped
- ½ teaspoon salt
- Freshly ground black pepper
- 1 tablespoon chopped fresh dill (optional)
- 1 egg
- 1 recipe Homemade Noodles dough (see page 78)

COOK'S TIP

KREPLACH CAN BE SERVED OTHER WAYS. COOK IN BOILING WATER AS DIRECTED AND SERVE TOSSED WITH BUTTER OR OIL AND GRATED CHEESE OR A TOMATO SAUCE. FOR A MAIN DAIRY MEAL, FRY KREPLACH IN BUTTER OR OIL AND A LITTLE CHOPPED ONION AND SPRINKLE WITH CHEESE.

☐ Into a food processor fitted with metal blade, process beef and chopped onion until finely chopped but not pasty. Add salt and pepper to taste, dill, if using, and the egg and, with pulse action, process until meat mixture is moist and holds together. Scrape into a bowl and refrigerate until ready to use.

☐ Prepare noodle dough and roll out as directed but do not leave to dry. Cut dough into 2-inch squares. Put 1 teaspoon filling in the center of each square and brush corners with a little water. Fold lower-left corner over upper-right corner to form a triangle, pressing the edges firmly together to seal.

☐ Transfer to a lightly floured cookie sheet and continue until all dough is used. (Kreplach can be made up to this point ahead and refrigerated until ready to cook.)

☐ Bring a large saucepot or kettle of water to a boil. Add some of the kreplach but do not overcrowd. Simmer gently 12 to 15 minutes. With a slotted spoon, remove and drain in a colander. Bring water back to a boil and continue until all kreplach are tender. (Cooked kreplach can be refrigerated or frozen for future use.)

☐ To serve, simmer kreplach in chicken or meat soup until heated through, 10 to 12 minutes. Serve piping hot.

CHEESE FILLING

COMBINE 2 CUPS COTTAGE CHEESE, 2 TABLESPOONS SOUR CREAM, 3 TABLESPOONS FINE BREAD CRUMBS OR MATZO MEAL, SALT AND PEPPER TO TASTE, 1 TABLESPOON CHOPPED FRESH PARSLEY, 1 TABLESPOON SNIPPED FRESH CHIVES AND 1 EGG. MIX WELL AND REFRIGERATE UNTIL READY TO SERVE.

KASHA VARNISHKES

6 TO 8 SERVINGS

Kasha, or roasted buckwheat groats, is a staple grain of poor Russian Jews because it is hearty and nourishing. There are two versions of this dish. The one eaten on Purim is a simple dish of sautéed onions with kasha and pasta bow ties. The original version, however, is like a little turnover, or varnishke, filled with kasha and mushrooms.

- 1 cup kasha
- 1 egg, lightly beaten
- ½ teaspoon salt
- Freshly ground black pepper
- 2 cups chicken or vegetable stock or water

- 1 tablespoon vegetable oil
- 3 cups coarsely chopped mushrooms
- 1 recipe Homemade Noodles dough (see page 78)
- Butter or oil for frying
- Sour cream for serving

☐ In a bowl combine kasha and beaten egg until kasha grains are well coated. Place kasha-egg mixture in a heavy-bottomed skillet and cook over medium heat until all grains are separate, 3 to 5 minutes.

☐ Sprinkle in salt and pepper to taste. Stir in chicken or vegetable stock or water and cook, over medium-low heat, for 10 minutes, adding a little more liquid if necessary.

☐ In a medium skillet, over medium-high heat, heat oil. Add mushrooms and cook until tender and most liquid is evaporated, 5 to 7 minutes.

☐ Uncover kasha and stir. Add cooked mushrooms and cook on medium-low heat until all liquid is absorbed, 3 to 5 minutes. Cool completely.

☐ Prepare noodle dough as directed but roll out into a large rectangle ⅛ inch thick. Using a 3-inch round cutter, cut as many dough circles as possible; reroll trimmings.

☐ Place 1 teaspoon kasha filling on to center of each dough circle. Brush the edge of dough with a little water and fold dough circle in half. Using a fork, press edges together to seal.

☐ Bring a large saucepot or kettle of water to a boil. Add the varnishkes and cook until tender, 12 to 15 minutes. Drain carefully in a colander. Serve in soup, with gravy, or fry in butter or oil and serve hot with sour cream.

ABOVE THE DATE HARVEST AT A KIBBUTZ IN THE BETH SHEAN VALLEY, ISRAEL.

> **EASY KASHA VARNISHKES**
>
> PREPARE KASHA AS ABOVE (WITH OR WITHOUT MUSHROOMS). FRY 1 FINELY CHOPPED ONION IN 2 TABLESPOONS BUTTER OR OIL UNTIL SOFT AND GOLDEN, 3 TO 5 MINUTES. STIR IN COOKED KASHA AND 1 CUP COOKED PASTA BOW TIES. TASTE FOR SALT AND PEPPER AND SERVE HOT, OR AS AN ACCOMPANIMENT TO MEAT DISHES.

FIDELLOS TOSTADOS

6 SERVINGS

Spanish Sephardic Jews have been eating a very thin vermicelli-like pasta called fidellos for centuries. It is also popular in Greece, introduced by Spanish Jews when they fled Spain during the Inquisition. I have often eaten this dish cooked by a Greek friend of mine, although he sometimes breaks the pasta coils and throws in rice as in this recipe.

- 1 12-ounce package vermicelli or angel hair pasta in coils
- ½ cup American long-grain rice
- ¼ cup olive oil
- 1 8-ounce can stewed tomatoes, drained
- 2 to 3 cups chicken stock or water
- 1 teaspoon salt
- ½ teaspoon dried oregano
- Freshly ground black pepper
- Fresh coriander leaves for garnish

☐ In a dry large heavy-bottomed skillet, over medium-high heat, heat pasta and rice until golden brown, stirring frequently, 5 to 7 minutes. (It does not matter if pasta breaks a little.)

☐ Add olive oil, tomatoes, chicken stock or water, salt, oregano and black pepper to taste. Bring to a boil; reduce heat to medium and simmer stirring often to unwind pasta, 7 to 10 minutes. Reduce heat to low, cover and cook 10 minutes longer until all the liquid is absorbed and pasta and rice are tender. Turn into a serving bowl and garnish with coriander leaves.

INDIAN RICE WITH TOMATOES AND SPINACH

6 SERVINGS

This is a mild, yet aromatic, rice dish from the Bene Israel Jewish community, near Bombay. Use fresh young spinach leaves if possible. Dhana jeera powder is a mixture of roasted and ground coriander and cumin seeds, available at Indian specialty stores.

- 3 tablespoons vegetable oil
- 1 onion, cut in half and thinly sliced
- 2 cups basmati or American long-grain rice, rinsed and soaked in cold water for 30 minutes
- 10 ounces young spinach leaves, cooked and squeezed dry, or 1 10-ounce package frozen spinach, thawed and squeezed dry
- 2 medium tomatoes, peeled, seeded and diced
- ¼ teaspoon turmeric
- 1 teaspoon dhana jeera powder (see above), or ¾ teaspoon ground coriander and ¼ teaspoon ground cumin
- Salt
- Freshly ground black pepper

☐ In a large heavy saucepan, over medium-high heat, heat oil. Add onion and cook until softened and golden, 5 to 7 minutes. Drain rice well and add to onion. Cook, stirring constantly, until rice turns translucent and begins to color, 1 to 2 minutes.

☐ Add spinach, tomatoes, turmeric and dhana jeera powder or coriander and cumin. Add salt and pepper to taste.

☐ Pour in 2 cups water and stir. Bring rice mixture to a boil, then cover tightly and reduce heat to very low. Cook until water is completely absorbed and rice is tender, 25 minutes.

☐ Remove cover and fluff rice gently with a fork being careful not to disturb the bottom layer which will have formed a crust. Cover and cook 10 minutes longer. Spoon rice into a serving bowl; scrape up browned crisp crust from bottom and spoon around the rice. Serve hot.

ROMANIAN-STYLE MAMALIGA

6 TO 8 SERVINGS

This classic cornmeal recipe is typical of Romanian-Jewish cooking and is similar to the northern Italian dish of polenta. Easily prepared, it makes an ideal accompaniment to braised meats with gravy, such as Old-fashioned Pot Roast with Onion Gravy (see page 58); the addition of cottage cheese makes it an ideal main dairy meal. Originally this was made with Brunza Alba, a Romanian cheese, but pot cheese, farmers' cheese or cottage cheese make adequate substitutes.

- 2 cups yellow cornmeal or polenta
- 1 teaspoon salt
- 4 tablespoons butter or oil (optional)
- 2 cups pot cheese, farmers' cheese or cottage cheese, drained and strained

☐ In a medium bowl, mix cornmeal or polenta with 1 cup cold water until smooth. Bring a large pot filled with 1 quart water to a boil. Add salt, then gradually pour in the moistened cornmeal, stirring constantly to prevent lumps.

☐ Over medium-low heat, cook, stirring constantly with a wooden spoon, until soft and all the water is absorbed, 20 to

35 minutes. Remove from heat and stir in butter or oil, if using, and the pot, farmers' or cottage cheese. Spoon into a serving bowl and serve immediately.

> ### VARIATION
>
> COOK CORNMEAL AS DIRECTED WITH 3 TO 3½ CUPS WATER AND STIR IN ONLY 2 TABLESPOONS BUTTER OR OIL. SPREAD EVENLY ON TO A LARGE COOKIE SHEET OR JELLY-ROLL PAN AND LEAVE TO COOL. WHEN FIRM, TURN OUT ON TO WORK SURFACE AND CUT INTO SQUARES. FRY IN MELTED BUTTER OR OIL; OR BRUSH WITH MELTED BUTTER OR OIL AND BROIL UNDER PREHEATED BROILER UNTIL HOT AND BROWNED, 3 TO 5 MINUTES. SERVE WITH ROAST MEATS AND POULTRY OR VEGETABLE STEWS.

ABOVE INDIAN RICE WITH TOMATOES AND SPINACH.

CHELOU

6 TO 8 SERVINGS

Chelou is a simple dish of steamed and baked rice or cooked on top of the stove in a way which forms a crust on the bottom and light fluffy rice above. This is an Iranian dish enjoyed by Jews and non-Jews alike and is traditional at Rosh Hashanah. Many other dishes use chelou as the base to which meat, vegetables or a stew of dried herbs and a little meat are added. Sometimes the baking dish or pan is lined with a thin layer of potatoes.

- 1 teaspoon salt
- 2 cups basmati or American long-grain rice, rinsed and soaked in cold water for 30 minutes
- 4 tablespoons oil, or 2 tablespoons oil and 2 tablespoons butter

☐ In a large, heavy-bottomed saucepot, over high heat, bring at least 2 quarts of water and salt to a boil. Drain rice in a strainer under cold running water until water runs clear. Add rice to boiling water and cook until a grain of rice feels almost tender, but is uncooked at center, 7 to 10 minutes. Stir occasionally being careful not to bruise rice. Drain rice into a strainer and rinse under warm running water to remove any starch. Drain well.

☐ In another large, heavy-bottomed saucepan or deep skillet with tight-fitting lid, over medium-high heat, heat 2 tablespoons oil with ¼ cup water until steaming. Spoon rice into the pan, shaking to distribute it evenly. Cover rice with a clean dry dish towel or double layer of paper towels. Cover pan tightly and reduce heat to very low. Cook 15 minutes, remove cover and cloth and, with the handle of a wooden spoon, poke several holes in the rice layer to allow steam to escape.

☐ Sprinkle over remaining 2 tablespoons oil mixed with 2 tablespoons water (see variation for method for butter), cover with cloth or paper towels, and cover tightly and cook 10 to 15 minutes longer.

☐ Uncover pan and remove dish towel or paper towels. Fluff rice gently with a fork, leaving bottom layer intact. Spoon rice into a serving bowl, then scrape the crusty layer from the bottom of the pan and spoon around the fluffy rice. Traditionally, honored guests got the crispy bits!

VARIATION

IF USING BUTTER FOR A DAIRY MEAL, MELT BUTTER IN 2 TABLESPOONS WATER AND PROCEED AS ABOVE. IF YOU WISH TO ADD POTATO LAYER, COOK RICE AS DIRECTED AND HEAT OIL (OR BUTTER) WITH WATER. COVER BOTTOM OF PAN WITH 2 MEDIUM POTATOES, PEELED AND CUT INTO ¼-INCH SLICES. COVER POTATOES WITH RICE AND PROCEED AS ABOVE. IN THIS VERSION IT IS POTATOES AND A LITTLE RICE WHICH FORM BOTTOM CRUST.

QUICK-AND-EASY COUSCOUS

4 SERVINGS

Couscous, a fine semolina made from wheat, is a staple food of North African Jews. It is eaten like rice in the Middle East or pasta in Italy. Once painstakingly slow to prepare, it is now very quick and easy thanks to the quick-cooking variety. It also makes a delightful change. Delicious on its own, it is also the perfect accompaniment for a lamb, beef or vegetable ragout. In North Africa, the couscous is generally steamed in a special piece of equipment called a *couscousier*. It is placed over the simmering stew to cook and then served with the meat or vegetables.

- ½ pound quick-cooking couscous
- 2 tablespoons olive oil
- 1 small onion, finely chopped
- 2 garlic cloves, finely chopped
- Salt
- Freshly ground black pepper
- 1 teaspoon red-pepper sauce, or ½ teaspoon cayenne pepper
- 1 teaspoon paprika
- 2 tablespoons chopped fresh parsley, coriander or mint

☐ Cook couscous according to manufacturers' directions. Set aside.

☐ In a medium skillet, over medium-high heat, heat oil. Add onion and cook until onion is soft and beginning to color, 3 to 5 minutes. Add garlic and cook 1 minute longer. Add salt and pepper to taste, red-pepper sauce or cayenne, paprika and chopped parsley, coriander or mint. Remove from heat and stir into cooked couscous. Serve hot or warm.

SALADS

Israeli Salad

Beet and Watercress Salad with Mustard Vinaigrette

German-Style Potato Salad

Moroccan Carrot Salad

Cucumber Salad with Dill

Tabbouleh

Avocado and Pomegranate Salad

ISRAELI SALAD

4 SERVINGS

This simple salad of diced fresh vegetables and olive oil is eaten everywhere in Israel, as an accompaniment to grilled chicken and meats, in pita pockets, and is even eaten for breakfast in some homes. You can add any vegetables you like, but tomato and cucumber are the essentials. The vegetables should be cut into very small dice, about ¼-inch pieces.

☐ In a large salad bowl, combine cubed tomato, diced cucumber, green pepper, onion and parsley; toss together.

☐ Sprinkle with olive oil, lemon juice and salt and pepper to taste; toss again. Garnish with fresh mint.

- 2 large ripe tomatoes, diced into ¼-inch cubes
- 1 large, or 2 small, cucumbers, peeled and diced
- 1 green pepper, cored, seeded and diced
- 1 onion, chopped
- 4 tablespoons chopped fresh parsley
- 2 to 3 tablespoons olive oil
- Juice of 1 lemon
- Salt
- Freshly ground black pepper
- Fresh mint leaves for garnish

VARIATION

PREPARE VEGETABLES AS ABOVE BUT DRESS WITH 3 TO 4 TABLESPOONS TAHINI, DILUTED WITH 2 TABLESPOONS LEMON JUICE AND SEASONED WITH SALT AND PEPPER. THIN TO THE DESIRED CONSISTENCY WITH A LITTLE WATER OR MORE LEMON JUICE.

BEET AND WATERCRESS SALAD WITH MUSTARD VINAIGRETTE

6 SERVINGS

Beets have always been a staple in the Russian-Jewish repertoire. They are also served in the Sephardic community with a simple dressing of lemon juice, olive oil and a little chopped fresh parsley or coriander. Here, fresh beets are combined with watercress and a classic mustard-based oil and vinegar dressing.

☐ Prepare vinaigrette. Into a small bowl, place wine vinegar. Add salt and pepper to taste and sugar, if using. Stir in mustard until well blended. With a wire whisk, slowly beat in oil or oils until vinaigrette is smooth and creamy. Set aside.

☐ Arrange watercress or spinach leaves on 6 individual plates. Evenly distribute sliced or diced beets among 6 plates. Stir vinaigrette and spoon some over each salad. Garnish with coriander leaves and serve immediately.

MUSTARD VINAIGRETTE

- 4 tablespoons white-wine vinegar
- Salt
- Freshly ground black pepper
- 1 teaspoon sugar (optional)
- 2 teaspoons Dijon-style mustard
- ⅔ cup olive oil or vegetable oil, or a combination

- 1 large bunch watercress, or 3 cups fresh young spinach leaves, trimmed and washed
- 10 to 12 small beets, cooked, peeled and thinly sliced or diced
- Fresh coriander leaves for garnish

GERMAN-STYLE POTATO SALAD

4 TO 6 SERVINGS

Although potatoes were not brought to Europe from South America until the 16th century, Jewish communities all over the world took to them in a short period of time. German Jews use potatoes extensively in breads, soups, and dumplings. They also enjoy them in kugels, latkes, and knishes, as well as boiled, fried, and roasted and in hot or cold potato salads. This is my mother's hot potato salad, a non-mayonnaise version.

- 2 pounds waxy potatoes, cooked, peeled and cut into ½-inch cubes
- 2 German-style dill pickles, diced
- 2 tablespoons vegetable oil
- 1 onion, finely chopped
- 1 garlic clove, finely chopped
- 1 stalk celery, peeled and finely chopped
- Salt
- Freshly ground black pepper
- 1 tablespoon light brown sugar
- 1 tablespoon German mustard
- ¼ cup red- or white-wine vinegar
- Chopped fresh parsley for garnish

☐ In a large bowl, place warm potatoes. Add diced dill pickles. Set aside.

☐ In a medium skillet, over medium-high heat, heat oil. Add onion, garlic and celery and cook until onion just begins to soften, 2 to 3 minutes. Add salt and pepper to taste. Stir in sugar, mustard and vinegar until well blended.

☐ Pour over potato-pickle mixture; toss gently to mix. Spoon into serving bowl and sprinkle with parsley for garnish. (If you like, drizzle with additional oil.)

MOROCCAN CARROT SALAD

4 TO 6 SERVINGS

This is a favorite Middle Eastern salad, popular in Israel. It is sweet and spicy, as well as being colorful. Raw grated carrots can be used, but traditionally the carrots are cooked first.

- 1 pound carrots, peeled and cooked until just tender, cooking liquid reserved
- 2 tablespoons vegetable oil
- 2 garlic cloves, peeled and finely chopped
- 1 teaspoon salt
- 1½ teaspoons cumin
- ½ teaspoon red-pepper flakes, cayenne pepper or red-pepper sauce
- 1 teaspoon sugar
- 2 to 3 tablespoons chopped fresh parsley
- 3 to 4 tablespoons lemon juice
- Fresh parsley sprigs for garnish

☐ In a food processor fitted with grater blade, or with a box grater, grate carrots into a large bowl. Set aside.

☐ In a medium skillet, over medium-low heat, heat oil. Add chopped garlic and cook until garlic begins to soften and color, 2 to 3 minutes. Add salt, cumin, red-pepper flakes, cayenne or red-pepper sauce and sugar, stirring to blend.

☐ Stir in chopped parsley and lemon juice. Slowly pour in ½ to ¾ cup of the carrot cooking liquid. Bring to a boil and simmer 3 to 5 minutes. Pour over carrots. Cool to room temperature.

☐ Cover and refrigerate 6 to 8 hours or overnight. Spoon into a serving bowl and garnish with parsley sprigs.

CUCUMBER SALAD WITH DILL

4 TO 6 SERVINGS

Cucumber salads are popular in most Jewish communities. In Eastern Europe, the preference is for a vinegar-based (or acetic-acid) marinade; in the Middle East, a yogurt base is used for tarator or cacik, traditional cucumber salads. Either way it is a delicious accompaniment to fish, poultry and lamb dishes and ideal on a buffet table.

☐ Into a 2-cup measure, pour vinegar and ½ cup water. Stir in sugar, salt and pepper to taste. Add chopped dill and stir; set aside.

☐ Using a fork, score the cucumber lengthwise. In a food processor fitted with a slicing disc, thinly slice cucumber. Place in a large bowl and pour marinade over. Refrigerate overnight. Serve chilled.

- ¼ cup white wine or white distilled vinegar
- 1 to 2 tablespoons sugar
- Salt
- Freshly ground black pepper
- 2 to 3 tablespoons finely chopped fresh dill
- 1 cucumber, lightly peeled

VARIATION

OMIT VINEGAR MARINADE. TO 1 CUP PLAIN YOGURT, ADD 1 CRUSHED GARLIC CLOVE, SALT AND PEPPER TO TASTE, 1 TO 2 TABLESPOONS LEMON JUICE AND 1 TABLESPOON CHOPPED FRESH DILL OR MINT. POUR OVER SLICED CUCUMBERS AND REFRIGERATE OVERNIGHT. SERVE CHILLED.

TABBOULEH

10 TO 12 SERVINGS

This Middle-Eastern cracked wheat salad is an ideal dish for a buffet party and makes a change from a rice salad. The cracked wheat has an earthy flavor enhanced by the abundant quantity of parsley – it is sometimes referred to as parsley salad. I first tasted this dish at a party in Paris given by an Israeli, and I have been serving it at parties ever since.

- 1 cup bulgur wheat
- 2 large ripe tomatoes, peeled, seeded and chopped, or 4 to 5 Italian plum tomatoes, finely chopped
- 1 small cucumber, peeled, seeded and finely chopped
- 4 scallions, finely sliced
- 4 to 6 tablespoons chopped fresh parsley
- 4 to 6 tablespoons chopped fresh mint
- Juice of 2 to 3 lemons
- ¾ cup olive oil
- Salt
- Freshly ground black pepper
- Vine leaves or shredded lettuce
- Cherry tomatoes, sliced olives and mint leaves for garnish

☐ In a large bowl, place bulgur wheat. Cover with cold water and leave to soak overnight or until tender.

☐ Drain in a colander or strainer. Turn on to a clean dish towel and roll in the towel to squeeze dry. Transfer to a large bowl and fluff with a fork.

☐ Add chopped tomatoes, cucumber, sliced scallions, chopped parsley and chopped mint; toss well to combine. Pour in lemon juice and olive oil and season to taste with salt and pepper. The flavor should be sharp and herby. Refrigerate until ready to serve.

☐ To serve, line a shallow bowl with prepared grape leaves or shredded lettuce. Pile bulgur wheat salad on to lettuce in a pyramid shape and surround with cherry tomatoes, sliced ripe olives and mint leaves.

AVOCADO AND POMEGRANATE SALAD

4 SERVINGS

Avocados are Israel's top export and so popular and plentiful they are used in many salads and appetizer dishes. Oranges, also a big export fruit, and pomegranates combine perfectly in this salad which makes an unusual first course or side dish for a meat or dairy dinner.

DRESSING
- 4 tablespoons white-wine vinegar
- 2 tablespoons orange juice
- Salt
- Freshly ground black pepper
- 1 teaspoon honey
- 2 tablespoons olive oil
- 1 tablespoon peanut or sunflower oil
- 2 tablespoons chopped fresh mint

- 1 ripe pomegranate, cut in half
- 1 cup black grapes, cut in half and seeded
- 2 ripe avocados
- 1 tablespoon lemon juice
- Fresh mint leaves to garnish

☐ In a small bowl, whisk together wine vinegar, orange juice, salt and pepper to taste and honey. Slowly whisk in olive oil and vegetable oil until dressing is thick and creamy. Stir in the chopped mint. Set aside.

☐ Into a medium bowl, scrape seeds out of pomegranate halves. Add grape halves and toss to mix.

☐ Cut avocados in half and remove seeds. Using a round-bladed knife, run it between skin and flesh of avocados, working skin away from flesh until skin is removed.

☐ Place avocados, round-side up, on work surface and, using a sharp knife and starting ½ inch below stem end, cut avocado lengthwise into ¼-inch slices, leaving stem end intact. Arrange each sliced avocado half on 4 individual plates. Using palm of hand, gently push avocado slices forward to fan out slices. Sprinkle lemon juice over them.

☐ Sprinkle one-quarter of the pomegranate seed-grape mixture on to each avocado half and spoon over dressing. Garnish each plate with a few mint leaves.

ABOVE AVOCADO AND POMEGRANATE SALAD.

DESSERTS

SUMMER FRUIT COMPOTE

OVEN-BAKED QUINCES

DRIED FRUIT COMPOTE

ISRAELI ORANGE SORBET

FRUIT-FILLED LOKSHEN PUDDING

FAVORITE MATZO PUDDING

SLICED EXOTIC FRUITS WITH DATES

SUMMER FRUIT COMPOTE

8 TO 10 SERVINGS

This is one of the easiest and most versatile summer desserts I know. It can be made with any combination of soft fruit and berries, but I try to use peaches, nectarines and apricots as a base. As the summer progresses, the choice of soft fruits and berries increases and, of course, cherries and grapes are wonderful additions. I always try to freeze some, as the sight of "fruit compote" thrills my husband on a cold winter's night. Compote should be served very cold with good fresh cream, whipped if you like. It is also delicious with vanilla ice cream. This is my mother-in-law's recipe.

- 6 ripe peaches, peeled and sliced
- 6 ripe nectarines or plums, sliced
- 6 ripe apricots, sliced
- 1 cinnamon stick (optional)
- Juice of 1 lemon
- ½ pound ripe black or sweet cherries
- 4 to 5 cups mixed berries, such as strawberries, cut in half if large, raspberries, blueberries, blackberries, boysenberries, loganberries or red currants
- Sugar or artificial sweetener
- Fresh mint leaves for garnish

☐ In a large nonaluminum saucepan, place sliced peaches, nectarines or plums and apricots. Add enough water to barely cover fruit, cinnamon stick (if using) and lemon juice. Over high heat, bring to a boil. Cover and cook over low heat 2 to 3 minutes; do not boil hard or fruit may break apart.

☐ Add cherries and cook, covered, until hard fruits are just tender and the cherries have begun to lose their color, 2 minutes longer. Add strawberries and cook 1 minute. Add remaining berries and cook, stirring occasionally, until hard fruits are tender and berries just beginning to soften, 2 to 3 minutes. Remove from heat and leave to stand, covered, for 30 minutes.

☐ Stir in sugar or artificial sweetener to taste. Transfer fruit to large serving bowl and refrigerate 3 to 4 hours or overnight. Garnish with fresh mint leaves.

OVEN-BAKED QUINCES

8 SERVINGS

Quinces are popular with North African and Middle Eastern Jews and, although they require lengthy cooking to tenderize them, they have a texture and perfume which is exotic and tempting.

- 1 cup lemon juice
- 4 quinces, trimmed, cut in half and cored it you like, but not peeled
- 2 cups sugar
- 1 cinnamon stick
- Rosewater for sprinkling
- Yogurt for serving (optional)

☐ In a shallow baking dish, place lemon juice. Place quince halves in dish, turning them to cover all sides with lemon juice to prevent them darkening.

☐ In a large, nonaluminum saucepot, place 1½ cups sugar and cinnamon stick. Stir in 1 quart water. Over high heat, bring to a boil, stirring to dissolve sugar.

☐ Gently add quinces and lemon juice and cook, covered, over low heat, until quinces are fork-tender, 20 to 25 minutes. Preheat oven to 450°F.

☐ Transfer quince halves, cut side up, to a medium baking dish; pour syrup over. Sprinkle quince halves with remaining sugar and bake, uncovered, until sugar caramelizes and the fruit is nicely browned and very tender, 7 to 10 minutes.

☐ Remove from oven and cool to room temperature. Sprinkle with a little rosewater and serve with yogurt if you like.

DRIED FRUIT COMPOTE

10 TO 12 SERVINGS

Fruit compotes made from dried fruit are popular with Jews from all over Europe. Throughout long winters, dried fruits were available and made a delicious dessert which could follow a milk or meat meal. Any combination of fruits can be used and the poaching liquid can range from water to tea, fruit juice or wine. You can experiment with this: serve with a dollop of yogurt or sour cream to cut the natural sweetness.

My family find the fruit yields enough sweetness, but you can add sugar or honey to taste. Use any combination of dried fruit you like, the bulk being prunes and apricots.

☐ Into a large nonaluminum saucepot, place prunes, apricots, pears, peaches, apple rings and raisins. Cover with 2 quarts water or enough to generously cover fruit.

☐ Stir in honey or sugar to taste, if using, and add grated lemon and orange zests and juices, cloves, cinnamon stick and peppercorns, if using. Over high heat, bring to a boil. Cook, covered, over low heat, until fruit is plump and tender, 20 minutes.

☐ With slotted spoon, remove cloves, cinnamon stick and peppercorns. Spoon fruit into a serving bowl and pour liquid over. Chill 3 to 4 hours or overnight. Sprinkle with toasted almonds for garnish and serve with yogurt or sour cream.

- 1 cup large pitted prunes
- 1 cup dried no-soak apricots
- 1 cup dried no-soak pears
- ½ cup dried no-soak peaches
- ½ cup dried no-soak apple rings
- ½ cup raisins
- ¼ cup honey or sugar (optional)
- Grated zest and juice of 1 lemon
- Grated zest and juice of 1 orange
- 4 to 6 whole cloves
- 1 cinnamon stick
- 1 tablespoon black peppercorns (optional)
- Slivered blanched almonds, toasted, for garnish

COOK'S TIP

IF YOU LIKE A THICKER SYRUP, REMOVE FRUIT TO A SERVING BOWL. RETURN LIQUID TO THE HEAT, BRING TO A BOIL AND REDUCE 4 TO 5 MINUTES. STRAIN OVER FRUIT AND CHILL AS ABOVE. SYRUP WILL THICKEN AS IT CHILLS.

ISRAELI ORANGE SORBET

6 SERVINGS

Citrus fruits are one of Israel's top exports and are available year round. Sorbets and ices are especially popular in the hot climate of the Middle East, as well as the rest of the world. Sorbet makes an ideal dessert choice after any meal – meat or milk – especially if you spoon a little Sabra, an Israeli chocolate-orange liqueur, over each serving.

- 1 cup sugar
- Grated zest and juice of 1 lemon
- Grated zest of 3 oranges
- 2 cups fresh-squeezed orange juice, strained
- 2 egg whites, beaten to soft peaks
- Fresh mint leaves for garnish
- Sabra (or other orange-flavor liqueur) for serving

☐ In a small heavy saucepan, combine sugar, lemon and orange zests and 1 cup water. Slowly bring to a boil, stirring until sugar dissolves. Cook 5 minutes; remove from heat and cool and refrigerate 3 to 4 hours or overnight.

☐ Combine lemon and orange juices with the chilled syrup and, if you like, strain for a very smooth sorbet.

☐ If using an ice-cream machine, freeze according to manufacturer's directions.

☐ Alternatively, put into a metal bowl and freeze 3 to 4 hours until semifrozen. Into a food processor fitted with metal blade, scrape the semifrozen mixture; process until light and creamy, 30 to 45 seconds. Return to metal bowl and freeze another 1½ hours. Scrape into food processor again and process with beaten egg whites until well mixed and light and creamy, 30 seconds. Freeze 3 to 4 hours until completely firm.

☐ Soften 5 minutes at room temperature before scooping into individual serving glasses. Garnish with a few mint leaves and pass liqueur, allowing each guest to pour a little over sorbet.

COOK'S TIP

ADDING BEATEN EGG WHITES GIVES SORBET A VERY SMOOTH, CREAMY TEXTURE. IF YOU PREFER A ROUGHER, "ICIER" TEXTURE, OMIT EGG WHITES. PROCESSING MIXTURE BREAKS UP THE ICE CRYSTALS AND CONTRIBUTES TO A SMOOTH TEXTURE.

FRUIT-FILLED LOKSHEN PUDDING

4 SERVINGS

A sweet kugel is an old-fashioned Ashkenazic dessert — rich
and heavy. This creamy version with dried fruits makes a
delicious change. Use vermicelli or angel hair pasta for a
very creamy pudding.

☐ In a medium saucepan, over medium-high heat, bring milk
to a boil. Add noodles and cook over low heat until noodles
are just tender and have absorbed most of the milk, 15
minutes, cool slightly.

☐ Preheat oven to 350°F. Lightly grease a 1-quart baking
dish or soufflé dish. In a large bowl, beat eggs, salt, lemon and
orange zests, cinnamon, nutmeg and sugar until well blended.
Add melted butter or margarine and dried fruits.

☐ Add cooked noodles to the egg mixture; toss together to
distribute the dried fruit evenly. Turn into the baking dish and
sprinkle with almonds. Bake until a knife inserted in to the
center comes out clean, 40 to 50 minutes.

- 2 cups milk
- ¼ pound vermicelli, angel hair pasta or thin spaghetti
- 2 eggs
- ¼ teaspoon salt
- Grated zest of 1 lemon
- Grated zest of 1 orange
- ½ teaspoon ground cinnamon
- ¼ teaspoon grated nutmeg
- ¼ cup sugar
- 2 tablespoons butter or margarine, melted
- ½ cup chopped no-soak dried apricots
- ¼ cup chopped pitted dates
- ¼ cup golden raisins
- ¼ cup slivered almonds

COOK'S TIP

FOR SOFTER, CREAMIER
PUDDING, BAKE PUDDING IN A
WATER BATH. PREPARE AS
ABOVE BUT PLACE BAKING
DISH OR SOUFFLÉ DISH INTO A
LARGER ROASTING PAN. FILL
PAN WITH BOILING WATER TO
COME ABOUT HALF WAY UP
SIDE OF BAKING DISH. COVER
FOR FIRST 25 MINUTES, THEN
UNCOVER TO BROWN TOP
AND ALMONDS.

FAVORITE MATZO PUDDING

6 SERVINGS

Made in the style of a noodle pudding, this pudding replaces the noodles with matzo, making it kosher for Passover. Mix in as many favorite ingredients and spices as you like: the expression "it's a real matzo pudding" means a real mix up or muddle! All ingredients should be kosher for Passover.

- 4 matzos, broken into small pieces
- 1 dessert apple or pear, peeled, cored and grated
- ½ cup raisins
- ¼ cup chopped no-soak dried apricots
- ½ cup chopped almonds or walnuts, toasted
- ⅓ cup sugar
- 1 teaspoon ground cinnamon

- ½ teaspoon grated nutmeg
- 1 tablespoon honey
- Grated zest and juice of 1 lemon
- 3 eggs
- 3 tablespoons fine matzo meal (cake meal)
- ½ cup pareve margarine
- 1 tablespoon sugar
- 2 tablespoons marmalade or apricot preserve

☐ Into a large bowl, place broken matzo pieces. Cover with cold water and leave to stand until slightly softened, 10 minutes. Drain well and mash with a fork until almost smooth.

☐ Preheat oven to 350°F. Lightly grease an 8- or 9-inch square, deep baking dish. Add grated apple or pear, raisins, apricots and almonds or walnuts to matzo and mix well. Stir in half the sugar, cinnamon, nutmeg, honey and lemon zest and juice.

☐ In a medium bowl, beat eggs with remaining sugar until thick and creamy and sugar is dissolved, 3 to 5 minutes. Beat into matzo mixture until well blended. Stir in half the melted margarine and scrape into the baking dish, smoothing top evenly.

☐ Drizzle remaining margarine over top and sprinkle with 1 tablespoon sugar. Bake until a knife inserted in the center comes out clean and top is browned and slightly puffed, 1 hour.

☐ In a small saucepan, over medium heat, heat marmalade or apricot preserve with 1 tablespoon water. When pudding is baked, brush mixture over the top and cool pudding at least 15 minutes before serving.

ABOVE A STREET VENDOR SELLING BAKED GOODS IN ISTANBUL, TURKEY.

SLICED EXOTIC FRUITS WITH DATES

6 SERVINGS

Fruit salad has always been a popular dessert in Jewish homes because it is neutral; it is welcome after meat or milk meals. Almost any seasonal fruits are delicious sliced or cut up together in their natural juices or with a fruit purée. This is not a traditional fruit salad, but a selection of exotic fruits, sliced and served together. Ogen melons from Israel are as sweet as sugar, as are the Israeli oranges. Dates are popular throughout the Middle East, but California produces a wonderful variety, the Medjool date, which I recommend for this dish.

- 1 Ogen melon, seeded and sliced in thin wedges and peeled
- 3 sweet seedless oranges, peeled and segmented, juice reserved
- 1 mango, peeled and thinly sliced
- 24 fresh lychees, peeled, or 1 16-ounce can lychees in their own juice
- 12 Medjool dates, cut in half lengthwise and pitted
- 1 pomegranate, cut in half, seeds reserved (optional)
- Fresh mint leaves for garnish

☐ Arrange slices of melon on each of 6 individual plates in a fan shape. Arrange peeled orange segments and mango slices in an attractive pattern over the melon slices.

☐ Evenly distribute fresh or canned lychees over fruit and sprinkle on some reserved juices from all fruits.

☐ Arrange 4 date halves on each plate and sprinkle over the pomegranate seeds, if using. Garnish with fresh mint leaves and serve.

Baked Goods

Lemon-Scented Plava

Easy Chocolate Passover Roulade

New York-Style Cheesecake

Lekach

"Jewish" Applecake

Sufganiyot

Coconut Macaroons

Hamantaschen

Easy Cinnamon Balls

Walnut-Raisin Rugelach

Moroccan Butter Cookies

Mandelbrot

Pecan-Cinnamon Buns

Quick-and-Easy Babke

Butter Kuchen

Bagels

Sesame Pita Bread

Kubaneh

Old-Fashioned Rye Bread

Challah

LEMON-SCENTED PLAVA

6 TO 8 SERVINGS

Passover cakes are probably the most uniquely Jewish of all cakes, because they are made with flour substitutes. These cakes were perfected by the Sephardic Jews in Spain who escaped to Greece during the Inquisition, but they are now enjoyed by Jews the world over. The most popular substitutes are potatostarch, very fine matzo meal sometimes called cake meal, and ground nuts. The end result is a light, delicate sponge cake, served here with a lemon sauce.

- 6 eggs, separated
- 1 cup sugar
- 1 cup fine matzo meal (cake meal)
- ½ cup finely ground blanched almonds or potato flour
- ¼ teaspoon ground cinnamon
- Grated zest and juice of 1 lemon
- Almond halves or slivered almonds for decoration

FOAMY LEMON SAUCE

- 1 tablespoon potatostarch
- ⅔ cup sugar
- Grated zest and juice of 1 lemon
- 2 eggs, separated

☐ Preheat oven to 350°F. Grease an 8½- to 9-inch springform pan. In a large bowl, with an electric mixer, beat egg yolks with half the sugar until thick and lemon colored and mixture forms a "ribbon" when beaters are lifted from bowl, 3 to 5 minutes.

☐ In another large bowl, with cleaned beaters, beat egg whites until soft peaks form. Gradually beat in remaining sugar, in 3 or 4 batches, beating well after each addition, until whites form stiff peaks.

☐ In a medium bowl, combine matzo meal, ground almonds or potato flour, cinnamon and lemon zest. Alternately, in 3 batches, fold beaten whites and matzo-almond mixture gently into the beaten yolks. Fold in lemon juice.

☐ Pour batter into prepared pan and press almond halves into batter at 2-inch intervals or sprinkle with slivered almonds.

☐ Bake until top is golden and skewer inserted in center comes out clean, 45 to 55 minutes. Remove to wire rack to cool 10 minutes. Carefully run a sharp knife around edge of pan to loosen edges, then unclip side of pan and remove. Cool completely; cake may sink a little.

☐ Prepare Foamy Lemon Sauce. In a medium saucepan, combine potatostarch and sugar. Slowly stir in 1½ cups water and lemon zest and juice, until well blended and smooth. Beat in egg yolks.

☐ Over medium-low heat, cook mixture until slightly thickened, 3 to 4 minutes. Bring to a boil, then remove from heat.

☐ In a medium bowl, with electric mixer, beat whites until soft peaks form. Slowly fold in yolk mixture until just blended. Cool, then refrigerate at least 1 hour or until chilled. Serve cold with cake.

EASY CHOCOLATE PASSOVER ROULADE

10 TO 12 SERVINGS

Sponge cakes are often served at Passover when leavening agents are not used. This easy cake is ideal for any time of the year. If you do not eat chestnuts, sweetened whipped cream or any favorite filling can be substituted.

- 6 squares (6 ounces) bittersweet or semisweet chocolate, chopped
- ¼ cup strong coffee
- 6 eggs, separated
- ⅓ cup sugar
- 2 teaspoons vanilla extract
- Cocoa powder
- Confectioners' sugar
- Candied chestnuts for garnish

CHESTNUT FILLING

- 2 cups heavy or whipping cream
- 2 tablespoons coffee-flavor liqueur, or 2 teaspoons vanilla or rum extract
- 2 cups canned sweetened chestnut purée

☐ Preheat oven to 350°F. Grease a 15½- × 10½-inch jelly roll pan; line with waxed paper or nonstick parchment paper, then grease and flour paper. In a small saucepan, over low heat, melt chocolate with coffee, stirring until smooth. Set aside and cool slightly.

☐ In a large bowl, with electric mixer, beat egg yolks with half the sugar until pale and thick, 4 to 5 minutes. Beat in cooled chocolate until just blended.

☐ In another bowl, with cleaned beaters, beat egg whites until soft peaks form. Gradually beat in remaining sugar, 1 teaspoon at a time, beating well after each addition until stiff peaks form. Beat in vanilla.

☐ Stir a large spoonful of whites into chocolate-yolk mixture to lighten it, then fold into remaining whites. Spoon into prepared pan, smoothing top evenly. Bake until cake springs back when lightly pressed with a finger, 12 to 15 minutes.

☐ Dust a clean dish towel with cocoa powder. When cake is baked, immediately turn out on to dish towel and remove paper. Starting at a narrow end, roll cake and towel together jelly-roll fashion. Remove to wire rack to cool completely.

☐ Make filling. In a large bowl, beat cream and liqueur or extract until soft peaks form. Beat a large spoonful of cream into chestnut purée to lighten it, then fold in remaining cream. Unroll cake and spread chestnut mixture to within 1 inch of edges. Using towel to lift cake, reroll cake jelly-roll fashion.

☐ Decorate roulade with bands of sifted confectioners' sugar. Carefully slide cake on to a long serving plate. If you like, decorate with candied chestnuts.

New York-Style Cheesecake

8 TO 10 SERVINGS

Baked cheese recipes can be traced back to the discovery of curd cheese in the Middle East centuries ago. Western cheesecake as we know it is probably a descendant of the Russian Easter pashka, a tall molded dessert of homemade cottage cheese, eggs, sugar, sour cream, butter and chopped nuts. This dense, smooth, lemony cheesecake is heavenly and perfect for a Shavuot dessert.

- 1½ cups crushed graham crackers (20–22 squares)
- ½ teaspoon ground cinnamon
- 3 tablespoons butter or margarine, melted
- 1½ pounds cream cheese
- ¾ cup sugar
- Grated zest of 1 lemon
- 1 teaspoon vanilla extract
- 3 eggs

SOUR CREAM TOPPING

- 1 cup sour cream
- 2 tablespoons sugar
- 1 teaspoon vanilla extract

☐ Preheat oven to 350°F. Lightly butter a 9-inch springform pan. In a medium bowl, combine graham cracker crumbs, cinnamon and butter or margarine. Press crumbs on to bottom and 1½ inches up sides sof pan. Bake 5 minutes until just set. Remove to a wire rack to cool.

☐ In a large bowl, with an electric mixer on medium-low speed, beat cream cheese with sugar until smooth. Add lemon zest and vanilla, then beat in eggs, 1 at a time, until batter is well blended and smooth.

☐ Carefully pour filling into cooled crust. Bake until firm at edges but still slightly soft in center, 45 to 50 minutes. Do not allow cake to brown; it should be puffed and slightly golden. Turn off oven and leave cheesecake in oven with door closed for 1 hour. (This helps prevent the surface from cracking.) Remove to wire rack, cool.

☐ Preheat oven to 425°F. Make topping. In a small bowl, combine sour cream, sugar and vanilla. Carefully pour over top of cake and return to oven. Bake 5 minutes. Remove cake to wire rack to cool completely. Refrigerate overnight.

☐ To serve, run a sharp knife around edge of pan to loosen edges. Carefully remove side of springform pan and place cake on serving dish.

ABOVE ONE OF THE MANY JEWISH FOOD EMPORIA IN NEW YORK CITY.

VARIATION

STRAWBERRY CHEESECAKE

PREPARE CHEESECAKE AS ABOVE, BUT BEFORE SERVING, DECORATE EDGE OF CAKE WITH STRAWBERRIES HULLED AND CUT IN HALF LENGTHWISE. IN A FOOD PROCESSOR FITTED WITH METAL BLADE, PROCESS 1 10-OUNCE PACKAGE FROZEN STRAWBERRIES IN LIGHT SYRUP, OR 1 POUND FRESH STRAWBERRIES, HULLED, AND 3 TABLESPOONS SUGAR TO TASTE. STRAIN AND ADD A LITTLE LEMON JUICE OR WATER TO THIN IF NECESSARY. SERVE SEPARATELY WITH CHEESECAKE.

LEKACH

12 SERVINGS

- 2½ cups all-purpose flour
- 1 cup whole-wheat flour
- ½ cup dark brown sugar
- 1 tablespoon baking powder
- 1 teaspoon baking soda
- 2 teaspoons ground ginger
- 1 teaspoon ground cinnamon
- ½ teaspoon ground allspice
- ½ cup chopped walnuts or almonds, toasted (optional)
- ½ cup golden raisins (optional)

- 1¾ cups good-quality natural honey
- 1 cup strong black coffee
- 3 tablespoons bourbon whisky, brandy or water
- 4 eggs
- ¼ cup vegetable oil
- ½ cup ginger preserve or chopped stem ginger in syrup
- Confectioners' sugar for dusting or honey for glazing

☐ Preheat oven to 350°F. Grease a 9- × 13-inch cake pan; line with waxed paper, then grease and flour paper.

☐ In a large bowl, combine flours, brown sugar, baking powder, baking soda, ginger, cinnamon and allspice. Stir in chopped walnuts or almonds and raisins if using. Set aside.

☐ In a small saucepan, over medium-low heat, heat honey with coffee until warm and remove from heat. Stir in bourbon whiskey, brandy or water.

☐ In a large bowl, beat eggs with vegetable oil until well blended. Beat in ginger preserve or stem ginger. Alternately, in 3 or 4 batches, stir warm honey mixture and flour mixture into the beaten egg mixture until well blended.

☐ Pour batter into prepared pan. Bake until skewer inserted in center comes out with just a few crumbs attached and top springs back when gently pressed with a finger, 1 hour. Remove tin to wire rack and cool completely.

☐ Turn out cake on to a rack and then back on to serving plate, so cake is right side up. Dust with confectioners' sugar or, if you do not mind a sticky cake, brush with slightly heated honey, and cut into squares to serve.

This honey cake is the traditional Jewish New Year's cake. Sweet honey as we know it did not really become available until Roman times and even then was prized for its medicinal uses and saved for joyful holidays and special occasions. Lekach, Yiddish for honey cake, or *pain d'épices* (spice bread) as it is called in France, is heavily flavored with ginger and other spices and resembles the German-style gingerbread, although that cake uses molasses instead of honey. This is my sister-in-law's recipe, the most popular in the family.

"JEWISH" APPLECAKE

16 TO 20 SERVINGS

Applecake made with oil is a popular choice for a Hannukkah cake because the oil symbolizes the holiday's miracle. These layers of tangy apples baked in a moist, sweet, lemon-scented batter is one of my favorite cakes. My sister-in-law uses this recipe, and I love it when she serves it at tea time.

APPLE FILLING
- 2 pounds tart cooking apples, peeled, cored and thinly sliced
- 4 tablespoons sugar
- 1 teaspoon ground cinnamon
- Grated zest and juice of 1 lemon

CAKE
- 4 eggs
- 1 cup superfine sugar
- 1 cup vegetable oil
- 2 cups self-rising cake flour, or 2 cups cake flour plus 2 teaspoons baking powder
- 1 teaspoon vanilla extract
- Sugar for sprinkling

☐ Preheat oven to 350°F. Grease a 9- × 13-inch cake pan. In a large bowl, toss apple slices with sugar, cinnamon, lemon zest and juice.

☐ In a large bowl, with electric mixer at medium speed, beat eggs with sugar until thick and lemon colored and mixture forms a "ribbon" when beaters are lifted from bowl, 3 to 5 minutes. Beat in oil until well blended. Stir in flour and vanilla just until well mixed and smooth.

☐ Pour half the batter into prepared pan. Spoon half the apple slices over batter. Cover apple slices with remaining batter; top with remaining apple mixture. Sprinkle with about 2 tablespoons sugar.

☐ Bake until apples are tender and cake is golden brown and puffed and top springs back when gently pressed with a finger, 1¼ to 1½ hours. Cover with foil during baking if top colors too quickly. Remove to wire rack to cool. Cut cake into squares and serve at room temperature.

SUFGANIYOT

24 DOUGHNUTS

These jelly- or jam-filled doughnuts were eaten by many Ashkenazic Jews in Central and Eastern Europe, and are now very popular in Israel at Hanukkah because they are fried in oil. Fried sweet fritters have a long history among Sephardic Jews and are probably descended from the Greek loukomades, a fritter which was dipped in a honey syrup.

- 2 packages active-dry yeast
- 2 tablespoons sugar
- 1¼ cups lukewarm milk
- 4 egg yolks
- 4 cups all-purpose flour
- ¼ teaspoon salt
- Vegetable oil for frying
- Plum, apricot, red currant or blackcurrant preserve
- Superfine sugar for coating

☐ In the bowl of an electric mixer fitted with dough hook, combine yeast, sugar and lukewarm milk. Stir 1 minute, then leave to stand until the surface begins to look bubbly and foamy, 10 to 12 minutes. With mixer on low speed, beat in egg yolks.

☐ Add flour and salt and mix until a soft dough forms. Knead until dough is smooth and elastic and clings to the dough hook, 4 to 6 minutes. Lightly grease a bowl and place dough in it, turn to coat dough with oil. (This prevents a crust from forming on surface of the dough.)

☐ Cover bowl with a clean dish towel and leave in a warm place until doubled in bulk, 1½ to 2 hours. Turn out dough on to floured surface and roll out about ¾ inch thick. Using a 2-inch floured cutter, cut out 24 or more circles. Dust with a little flour and cover with dish towel; leave until puffy and risen, 20 to 30 minutes. (Knead scraps together and return to bowl for 20 to 30 minutes to rise again; reroll and cut.)

☐ Fill a deep-fat fryer or large saucepan with 3 inches oil and, over medium-high heat, heat to 350° to 360°F. Fry doughnuts in batches 3 to 4 minutes on each side. Do not crowd or temperature of oil will drop and doughnuts will absorb too much oil. With a slotted spoon, remove to paper towels to drain.

☐ Fill a small pastry bag fitted with a ½-inch plain tip with preserve. When cool enough to handle, make a small slit in side of each doughnut. Insert tip into a doughnut and squeeze about 1 teaspoon of the preserve into center.

☐ Into a small shallow dish, place ½ cup sugar. Roll each filled doughnut in the sugar to coat on all sides. Serve warm.

ABOVE MAGNIFICENTLY LIT INTERIOR OF AN OLD SYNAGOGUE IN MOSCOW.

COCONUT MACAROONS

ABOUT 30 MACAROONS

These are an easy Passover cookie, very popular in the United States as they store well and taste delicious. Of course, all macaroons are a good way to use extra egg whites.

- 4 egg whites
- ¼ teaspoon cream of tartar
- 1 cup sugar
- 1 teaspoon lemon juice or distilled white vinegar
- 1 teaspoon vanilla extract
- 2½ cups moist, unsweetened shredded coconut.

☐ In a large bowl, with electric mixer at medium speed, beat whites until frothy. Add cream of tartar and beat on high speed until firm peaks form. Gradually sprinkle in sugar, 2 tablespoons at a time, beating well after each addition until whites form stiff peaks.

☐ Sprinkle lemon juice or vinegar, vanilla and coconut over whites. Gently fold in until just blended.

☐ Preheat oven to 300°F. Line 2 large cookie sheets with nonstick parchment paper or foil. Drop mixture by heaping teaspoonsful, keeping a cone shape, about 1 inch apart.

☐ Bake 40 to 45 minutes until lightly browned; macaroons should be *very* slightly soft in center. Remove macaroons on paper to wire rack to cool slightly. Carefully peel off paper and cool completely. Store in an airtight container.

HAMANTASCHEN

ABOUT 30 COOKIES

Also called "haman's ears," these are little three-cornered cookies which have become the traditional Ashkenazic Purim sweet. They can be made from a yeast-based dough or an easy cookie-dough base. The most traditional fillings are poppy seeds or prunes.

COOKIE DOUGH
- ⅔ cup (1 stick plus 2 tablespoons) unsalted butter or margarine, softened
- ½ cup sugar
- 1 egg
- 3 tablespoons milk or water
- ½ teaspoon vanilla extract
- 2 to 2¼ cups all-purpose flour
- 1 teaspoon baking powder

POPPY SEED-HONEY FILLING
- 2 cups poppy seeds, whole or ground
- ½ cup honey
- ¼ cup light brown sugar
- ⅛ teaspoon salt
- ¼ cup finely chopped walnuts or blanched almonds (optional)
- 1 tablespoon lemon juice
- ½ teaspoon grated lemon zest
- 1 egg, beaten, for glaze (optional)

> **VARIATION**
>
> **PRUNE-FILLED HAMANTASCHEN**
>
> SOMETIMES CALLED LACQUA, THIS IS REALLY A PRUNE BUTTER. COMBINE 1½ TO 2 CUPS CHOPPED PITTED PRUNES, GRATED ZEST AND JUICE OF 1 ORANGE AND 1 CUP WATER IN A MEDIUM SAUCEPAN. COOK OVER MEDIUM HEAT UNTIL SOFT, 5 MINUTES. REMOVE FROM HEAT AND COOL SLIGHTLY. MASH PRUNE MIXTURE BY HAND OR PURÉE IN A FOOD PROCESSOR FOR FINE PASTE. STIR IN 2 TABLESPOONS PLUM OR APRICOT PRESERVE. PREPARE DOUGH AND FILL AND BAKE AS ABOVE.

☐ In a medium bowl, with electric mixer, cream butter or margarine and sugar until smooth and well blended. Add egg, milk or water and vanilla and beat until smooth and creamy.

☐ Combine flour and baking powder, then gently stir into butter-mixture until well blended.

☐ Turn out dough on to lightly floured surface and knead lightly to blend. Form into a ball, flatten and wrap tightly. Refrigerate until completely firm, 3 to 4 hours or overnight.

☐ Make filling. In a medium saucepan, over medium-low heat, cook poppy seeds, ½ cup water, honey, brown sugar and salt until thickened to a soft pastelike consistency, stirring frequently, 5 minutes. Remove from heat and cool slightly. Stir in chopped nuts, if using, and lemon juice and zest.

☐ Preheat oven to 375°F. Lightly grease 2 large cookie sheets. Place dough on lightly floured surface and cut in half; refrigerate one half. Roll out dough ⅛-inch thick. Using a 2-inch round cutter, cut as many circles as possible. Lightly brush edge of dough with water and place 1 teaspoon poppy seed filling in center of each. Pull up edges in three equidistant places to form a triangle. Pinch edges together, leaving a tiny space open along each side.

☐ Place dough triangles on cookie sheet about 1-inch apart. Brush with the egg glaze, if you like. Bake until golden brown, 14 to 18 minutes. Remove to wire rack to cool. Repeat with remaining dough. Store cookies in an airtight container.

ABOVE SCUBA DIVING AND WINDSURFING IN THE RED SEA, ISRAEL.

EASY CINNAMON BALLS

ABOUT 20

These cookies were so easy my brothers and I were allowed to make them when we were quite young. We could not go close to the oven and the size of the cookies was never uniform, but we all had a good time; part of the joy of Passover.

- 2 cups finely ground blanched almonds or walnuts
- 1 cup sugar
- 1 tablespoon ground cinnamon
- 2 egg whites
- ⅛ teaspoon cream of tartar
- Confectioners' sugar and cinnamon for rolling

☐ Preheat oven to 325°F. Lightly grease a large cookie sheet. In a medium bowl, combine ground almonds or walnuts, ½ cup sugar and cinnamon. Set aside.

☐ In another medium bowl, with electric mixer, beat whites until frothy. Add cream of tartar and continue beating until soft peaks form. Gradually add remaining sugar, 1 tablespoonful at a time, beating well after each addition, until whites are stiff and glossy. Gently fold in nut mixture.

☐ With wet hands, shape mixture into walnut-size balls. Place on cookie sheet about 1 inch apart. Bake until golden brown and set, 25 to 30 minutes. Remove cookie sheet to wire rack to cool slightly.

☐ In a small bowl, combine ½ cup confectioners' sugar and ¼ teaspoon cinnamon until well blended. Roll each warm ball in mixture to coat, then set on wire rack to cool completely. Add more confectioners' sugar and cinnamon if necessary. When cold, roll each ball again in sugar mixture.

COOK'S TIP

IF MIXTURE IS TOO SOFT TO ROLL, ADD A LITTLE MORE GROUND ALMOND OR A LITTLE FINE MATZO MEAL TO STIFFEN IT.

WALNUT-RAISIN RUGELACH

ABOUT 60 PIECES

Rugelach are one of the most popular Jewish pastries in the United States. Often made with a simple cream cheese pastry, these little filled crescents melt in the mouth. Crescent-shaped cookies became very popular in Vienna as the shape became the symbol of Austrian victory over the Turks, in the late 17th century, but this cookie may well have its origins in the Middle East and Sephardic communities. The fillings can vary from poppy seed to cinnamon and walnuts, to cheese or chocolate or commonly raspberry or apricot preserves.

CREAM CHEESE PASTRY

- 1 cup (2 sticks) unsalted butter, softened
- ½ pound cream cheese, softened
- 1 tablespoon sugar
- 2 to 3 tablespoons sour cream
- 2 cups all-purpose flour
- ¼ teaspoon salt

FILLING

- ¾ cup golden raisins
- 1 cup finely chopped walnuts
- 2 teaspoons ground cinnamon
- ⅓ cup sugar

- Milk for glazing
- 2 tablespoons sugar mixed with ½ teaspoon cinnamon for sprinkling

☐ In a large bowl with electric mixer (or by hand), cream butter and cream cheese together until well blended. Add sugar and beat until smooth, then beat in sour cream and mix in flour and salt until a soft dough is formed. Shape into a ball and flatten to disc. Wrap dough well and refrigerate until dough is firm, at least 2 hours.

☐ Preheat oven to 350°F. Lightly grease 2 large cookie sheets. In a small bowl, toss raisins and walnuts with the cinnamon and sugar to mix. Set aside.

☐ Place dough on lightly floured surface and cut into quarters; work with one-quarter at a time, keeping remaining dough refrigerated. Roll out one-quarter of the dough ⅛ inch thick. Using a 10-inch plate or bottom of 10-inch tart pan, cut dough into a 10-inch circle. Sprinkle dough with about one-fifth of the filling to within 1 inch of the edge.

☐ With a long-bladed, sharp knife, cut dough circle into 10- to 12-equal wedges. Starting at the curved edge, roll up each wedge jelly-roll fashion. Place each on cookie sheet, point side down (to keep filling from escaping) about 1 inch apart, curving ends down to form a crescent shape.

☐ Brush each crescent with a little milk and sprinkle with a little sugar-cinnamon mixture.

☐ Bake until golden brown, 20–25 minutes. Remove cookies to a wire rack to cool. Repeat with remaining dough and reroll trimmings to make extra cookings. Store in an airtight container.

VARIATIONS

RASPBERRY-ALMOND RUGELACH

COMBINE 1 CUP GROUND BLANCHED ALMONDS WITH 1 CUP RASPBERRY PRESERVE. SPREAD ONE-FIFTH OF MIXTURE ON DOUGH CIRCLE BEFORE CUTTING INTO WEDGES TO WITHIN 1 INCH OF EDGE. SHAPE AND BAKE AS ABOVE.

POPPY SEED RUGELACH

USE 1¼ CUPS CANNED POPPY SEED FILLING, SPREADING ABOUT ONE-FIFTH ON EACH DOUGH CIRCLE BEFORE CUTTING. SHAPE AND BAKE

MOROCCAN BUTTER COOKIES

ABOUT 30 COOKIES

Butter cookies flavored with nuts are found in most national cuisines from Morocco to Mexico. The Greek kourabiedes, or shortbread snowball, are made with almonds; the Austrian kipferl is made with hazelnuts. These cookies, eaten in Morocco on Purim, can be made with walnuts or almonds.

- 1 cup (2 sticks) unsalted butter, softened
- 1 cup sugar
- 3 cups all-purpose flour
- ⅓ cup finely ground walnuts or almonds
- Coarsely chopped walnuts to decorate (optional)

☐ In a large bowl, with an electric mixer, beat butter until white and creamy, 5 to 7 minutes. Add sugar and continue beating until very smooth and creamy, 4 to 5 minutes. Stir in flour and ground walnuts or almonds by hand until well blended and a soft dough is formed. If dough is too soft to handle, add a little more flour or chill until dough is firm enough to handle, 30 minutes.

☐ Preheat oven to 300°F. Lightly flour large cookie sheets, but do not grease. With lightly floured hands, divide dough into walnut-size pieces and roll into smooth balls. Place on cookie sheets about 1 inch apart. Press a few walnuts on top of each ball.

☐ Bake until set, 20 to 30 minutes. Do not let cookies overcook or brown at all; they should remain a creamy off-white color. Remove to a wire rack to cool. Store in an airtight container.

MANDELBROT

ABOUT 36

Mandelbrot, meaning almond bread in Yiddish, are hard, almond cookies, double baked to create a dry cookie like the Italian *biscotti alla mandorla*. It is likely that this cookie was introduced to the Italians by the Spanish Jews. These cookies are delicious with coffee or tea, or as in Italy with a sweet dessert wine – *vino santo*.

- 2½ cups all-purpose flour
- 2 teaspoons baking powder
- ¼ teaspoon salt
- 3 eggs
- 1 cup sugar
- 6 tablespoons vegetable oil
- Grated zest of 1 lemon
- 1 teaspoon lemon juice
- ½ teaspoon almond extract
- 1 cup coarsely chopped blanched or slivered almonds

☐ Preheat oven to 350°F. Grease 2 cookie sheets. In a medium bowl, sift flour, baking powder and salt. Set aside.

☐ In a large bowl, with electric mixer, beat eggs with sugar until thick and creamy, 3 to 5 minutes. Beat in oil, lemon zest and juice and almond extract. With the mixer on low speed, slowly add flour mixture until blended. Stir in almonds and beat until the dough is smooth.

☐ Turn out dough on to lightly floured surface and knead lightly. Divide dough in half and form into 2 long, flat loaves about 3 inches wide and 1¼ inches high. Place 1 loaf on each cookie sheet and bake until golden brown, 35 to 40 minutes.

☐ Remove loaves from oven and leave to cool 10 to 15 minutes. When cool enough to handle, carefully cut ½-inch diagonal slices, dough will be soft inside. Wipe cookie sheets and return slices to cookie sheet (you will need to bake in batches). Bake until golden brown on underside, 6 to 7 minutes, then turn slices; bake another 5 to 7 minutes until golden. Remove to wire rack to cool completely. Store in an airtight container.

PECAN-CINNAMON BUNS

16 SERVINGS

These buns form a sweet, sticky, delicious coffeecake. They come from the German-Austrian tradition of yeast cakes but have become popular all over the U.S. as a coffee-break treat. This is my brother's favorite.

- 1 packet active-dry yeast
- 2 tablespoons sugar
- ¼ cup lukewarm water
- ⅓ cup milk
- 2 tablespoons butter or margarine
- ¼ teaspoon salt
- 1 egg, well beaten
- 2 teaspoons vanilla extract
- 2 cups all-purpose flour

PECAN-CINNAMON MIXTURE
- 3 tablespoons butter or margarine, melted
- ¼ cup light corn syrup
- ⅔ cup light brown sugar
- 1 teaspoon ground cinnamon
- ½ cup coarsely chopped pecans
- ½ cup golden raisins

☐ In the bowl of an electric mixer fitted with dough hook, combine yeast, 1 tablespoon sugar and lukewarm water. Stir until yeast begins to dissolve, 1 minute. Leave to stand until bubbles begin to form on the surface and mixture looks foamy, 7–10 minutes.

☐ In a small saucepan, over medium heat, heat milk, butter or margarine, remaining sugar and salt; bring just to a boil. Cool to lukewarm. Stir into the yeast mixture. With machine on low speed, beat in egg and vanilla. Slowly add flour until mixture forms a smooth dough. On medium speed, beat dough until smooth and elastic, 3 to 4 minutes.

☐ Lightly grease a bowl and place dough in bowl; turn dough to coat. (This prevents a crust from forming on the surface.) Cover with clean dish towel and leave in a warm place until dough doubles in bulk, 1 to 1½ hours.

☐ Grease a 9-inch square baking dish or pan with half the melted butter, for filling, and drizzle with half the corn syrup. In a small bowl, combine brown sugar and cinnamon, then sprinkle half over butter and corn syrup in bottom of dish. Sprinkle with half the pecans.

☐ Turn out dough on to lightly floured surface and knead lightly. Roll out dough into an 8- × 16-inch rectangle. Spread dough with remaining butter, drizzle with remaining corn syrup and sprinkle with remaining sugar mixture, pecans and raisins. Starting at one long side, roll up dough jelly-roll fashion.

☐ With a sharp knife, slice "jelly-roll" into 1-inch slices and place, cut side down, in dish. Cover with dish towel and leave in a warm place until doubled in bulk, 1 hour. Preheat oven to 325°F.

☐ Bake 35 to 40 minutes until rolls pull away from side of tin. Remove to wire rack to cool 2 minutes, then turn out on to a shallow pan or serving dish. Using a fork, separate individual rolls from each other. Serve buns warm.

Quick-and-Easy Babke

8 SERVINGS

Babke is an egg-rich yeast dough of Russian-Polish origins. A yeast cake of this type probably exists in every country; it certainly resembles the German kugelhuph, the Spanish bola and what Italian Jews call bollo. In any language, studded with raisins, nuts and candied peel, this makes a delicious tea or coffee bread. This is a very easy no-knead recipe, moistened with a rum syrup. (You may notice the resemblance to the French *Baba au Rhum*!)

- ½ cup milk
- ¼ cup sugar
- 1 package active-dry yeast
- ¼ cup (½ stick) butter or margarine, softened
- 3 eggs
- 1 teaspoon vanilla or rum extract
- 2⅓ cups all-purpose flour
- ¼ cup chopped almonds or walnuts

- ¼ cup raisins, soaked in hot water 10 minutes and drained
- ¼ cup candied orange or lemon peel

RUM SYRUP
- ½ cup sugar
- 2 teaspoons rum or vanilla extract

☐ In a small saucepan, over medium heat, heat milk and sugar until bubbles form around edge of pan and sugar is dissolved, stirring frequently. Cool to lukewarm.

☐ In a large bowl of an electric mixer, combine yeast and half the milk-sugar mixture. Stir until yeast begins to dissolve, 1 minute. Stir in remaining milk and butter or margarine; it does not need to melt.

☐ With mixer at low speed, beat in eggs, vanilla or rum extract and flour; continue to beat until batter is soft and smooth. Cover bowl with clean dish towel and leave in a warm place until well risen, 1 to 1½ hours.

☐ Grease and flour a 9- or 10-inch tube pan. With a wooden spoon or palm of your hand, beat almonds or walnuts, raisins and candied orange or lemon peel into dough. Turn into prepared pan.

☐ Cover with dish towel and leave in a warm place until dough has risen almost to top of pan, 50 to 60 minutes. Preheat oven to 350°F.

☐ Bake until top is golden brown and feels firm to the touch, 30 to 40 minutes.

☐ Meanwhile, make syrup. In a small saucepan, over high heat, combine sugar with ½ cup water and bring to a boil, stirring to dissolve sugar. Remove from heat and stir in rum or vanilla extract.

☐ When cake is baked, remove to wire rack and with a fork immediately pierce top all over. Slowly pour syrup over the cake while still hot.

☐ Leave cake to stand until syrup is absorbed, 1 hour. Carefully remove cake to serving plate and serve warm or at room temperature.

ABOVE NOTE THE STAR OF DAVID ON THE WALL OF THIS JEWISH YEMINI HOME, SAMALA, NORTH YEMEN.

BUTTER KUCHEN

10–12 SERVINGS

Kuchen, Austrian-German-style coffeecakes, epitomize the type of cake preferred by the Central and Eastern European Jews. Taken to the United States by German immigrants, the best ones are still the ones found in old German-Jewish bakeries.

- 2 packages active-dry yeast
- ¾ cup sugar
- ¼ cup lukewarm milk
- ¾ cup (1½ sticks) unsalted butter or margarine, softened
- 3 eggs, lightly beaten
- 1 cup sour cream
- Grated zest of 1 lemon
- 1 teaspoon vanilla extract
- 5½ cups flour
- 1 teaspoon salt

FILLING
- 3 tablespoons butter or margarine, melted
- 1 tablespoon ground cinnamon
- ¾ cup sugar
- 1 cup golden raisins
- ½ cup candied lemon peel

GLAZE
- 3 to 4 tablespoons confectioners' sugar
- 1 to 2 teaspoons lemon juice

☐ In a small bowl, combine yeast, 2 tablespoons sugar and lukewarm milk. Stir until yeast begins to dissolve, 1 minute. Leave to stand until bubbles form on the surface and mixture looks foamy, 7 to 10 minutes.

☐ In bowl of an electric mixer fitted with beaters, cream butter or margarine and remaining sugar until well blended and smooth, 2 to 3 minutes. Beat in eggs, sour cream, lemon zest, vanilla and yeast mixture.

☐ Scrape beaters and replace with dough hook. On low speed, slowly add flour and salt and beat until well blended and a soft dough forms. Increase speed to medium and knead dough until dough is smooth and elastic, 5 to 7 minutes.

☐ Lightly grease bowl. Place dough in bowl and turn to coat. (This prevents dough from forming a crust.) Cover bowl with a damp dish towel and leave in a warm place until doubled in bulk, 2 to 2½ hours. (Alternatively, cover bowl with dish towel and refrigerate overnight to allow dough to rise very slowly.)

☐ Lightly grease a large cookie sheet. Turn out dough on to lightly floured surface and roll dough ½ inch thick into a rectangle at least 24 inches long; brush with melted butter for filling. In a small bowl, combine cinnamon and sugar, then sprinkle over dough. Sprinkle with raisins and candied lemon peel.

Starting at one long end, roll up dough jelly-roll fashion and bring ends together. Pinch ends to form a ring and place on cookie sheet. With a sharp knife or scissors, slash ring diagonally from outer edge halfway to center edge at 3-inch intervals. (This allows dough to rise more evenly, shows filling and forms a decorative shape.) Cover with dish towel and leave in warm place until ring doubles in bulk, 1½ to 2 hours.

☐ Preheat oven to 375°F. Bake until golden brown, 40 to 45 minutes. Remove kuchen to wire rack to cool.

☐ Into a small bowl, sift confectioners' sugar. Stir in 2 tablespoons water and lemon juice to form a glaze. Thin with a little more water if necessary. Drizzle over warm kuchen and slide on to serving plate. Serve warm.

BAGELS

1 DOZEN

Bagels are round rolls with a hole in the middle, symbolizing the continuous circle of life. It is difficult to trace the bagel's origin, but it is likely they are from Poland or Austria as the word bagel could derive from the Austrian/German word *beugel*, meaning stirrup, or the German/Yiddish *beugel*, meaning a curved ring or bracelet. Whatever its origin, it is surely one of the most popular "Jewish" breads, eaten all over the United States for breakfast, brunch or snacks. It is most popular with cream cheese and lox, but nowadays it is home to just about any sandwich filling.

The original plain bagel (water bagel) is made from high-gluten flour and is lightly poached in water to reduce its starch content before being glazed and baked; this gives the bagel its distinct, chewy texture. The addition of eggs to the dough was an American idea, as are the variety of flavors, such as pumpernickel, cinnamon-raisin, poppy or sesame seed, onion, garlic or pizza! In the U.S. there are bagel bakeries in all big cities, some open 24 hours. In Canada, the dispute for the best bagel rages on between Montreal and Toronto.

In London, I think the best bagels still come from the East End. The old Jewish neighborhood has just about disappeared, replaced by Bangladeshi immigrants, but one shop still remains, selling the old-fashioned, chewy-style bagel.

- 1 package active-dry yeast
- 2 tablespoons sugar
- ¼ cup vegetable oil or margarine
- 1 teaspoon salt
- 4 cups all-purpose flour
- 1 egg, lightly beaten (optional)
- 1 egg, well beaten, for glaze
- Poppy or sesame seeds (optional)

VARIATION

BAGEL CHIPS

SLICE DAY-OLD BAGELS LENGTHWISE, INTO THIN SLICES ABOUT ¼ INCH THICK. BRUSH WITH MELTED BUTTER OR OIL AND SPRINKLE WITH SESAME OR POPPY SEEDS IF YOU LIKE. BAKE ON A GREASED COOKIE SHEET IN A PREHEATED 375°F OVEN UNTIL BROWNED AND CRISP, 4 TO 5 MINUTES. REMOVE TO WIRE RACK TO COOL. STORE IN AN AIRTIGHT CONTAINER AND SERVE AS THEY ARE OR WITH DIPS.

☐ In a small bowl, combine yeast and 1 tablespoon sugar. In a small saucepan over medium heat, heat remaining sugar, vegetable oil or margarine and salt with 1 cup water, stirring until blended. Pour into yeast-sugar mixture and stir until dissolved, 1 to 2 minutes. Leave to stand until surface becomes bubbly, 5 to 7 minutes.

☐ Into a food processor fitted with metal blade, place flour. With machine running, slowly pour liquid into flour until mixture forms a ball of dough. If using an egg, add egg with liquid. Continue to process 1 minute longer. Dough should be smooth and not sticky. Add a little more flour if dough is too soft and process 30 seconds longer.

☐ Lightly oil a bowl and place dough in bowl; turn to coat dough. (This prevents a crust from forming on the surface.) Cover bowl with a clean dish towel and leave in a warm place to rise until doubled in bulk, 1½ to 2 hours.

☐ Turn out dough on to lightly floured surface and knead 2 to 3 minutes. Divide dough into 12 equal-size pieces. Roll each piece into a log about 5½ inches long; wet one end slightly and shape into a ring, pressing ends together firmly. Arrange rings on a large lightly floured cookie sheet. Cover with dish towel and leave to rise until almost doubled in size, 20 to 30 minutes.

☐ Preheat oven to 400°F. Bring a large stockpot or kettle filled with water over high heat, to a gentle boil. Carefully slide 3 or 4 bagels into the water and cook 1 minute. Remove to paper towel and drain; continue cooking bagels.

☐ Lightly grease 2 large cookie sheets. Arrange 6 boiled bagels on each sheet and brush with a little egg glaze and sprinkle with poppy or sesame seeds, if using. Bake bagels until well browned and crisp, 20 minutes. Remove to wire rack to cool. Serve warm or cool completely, then reheat to serve if you like.

SESAME PITA BREAD

ABOUT 1 DOZEN

Pita, sometimes called pocket bread, is a Middle-Eastern flatbread. In the Middle East it is baked fresh everywhere; in the U.S. and Great Britain it is increasingly popular because of the large Greek and Indian communities. To get the effect of being baked in a clay oven, use a hot griddle or cast-iron skillet. This is an ideal bread for weight-watchers as it does not contain any fat, but is full of flavor, especially this sesame version.

- 4 cups all-purpose or white bread flour
- 1 teaspoon salt
- 1 package active-dry yeast
- 1 teaspoon sugar
- 1½ cups lukewarm water
- Sesame seeds for rolling

> **COOK'S TIP**
>
> TO HEAT STORE-BOUGHT PITAS, PLACE ON A COOKIE SHEET AND BAKE IN A PREHEATED 400°F OVEN 2 TO 3 MINUTES UNTIL HOT AND PUFFED.

☐ In a food processor fitted with metal blade, process the flour and salt 2 to 3 seconds to combine.

☐ In a 4-cup measure or medium bowl, combine yeast, sugar and ½ cup lukewarm water, stirring, until yeast is almost dissolved, 1 to 2 minutes. Leave to stand until surface looks bubbly and foaming, 10 to 12 minutes.

☐ Stir 1 cup lukewarm water into yeast mixture. With machine running, gradually pour in yeast liquid. If dough looks too dry, add a little water, 1 tablespoon at a time, and process until a ball of dough forms. Process 1 minute longer.

☐ Lightly oil a bowl, place dough in bowl and turn to coat with oil. (This prevents a crust from forming on the surface.) Cover dough with damp dish towel and leave to rise in a warm place until doubled in bulk, 1½ to 2 hours.

☐ Turn out dough on to lightly floured surface and knead lightly. Roll dough into a long, thick log and cut into about 12 equal-size pieces. Roll each piece into a smooth ball, flouring the surface only if necessary. Place balls on a floured cookie sheet and cover with the dish towel. Leave to rise until doubled in bulk, about 30 minutes.

☐ In a small bowl, pour about ½ inch sesame seeds. Roll each ball into the sesame seeds to coat well; add more seeds to bowl as needed. On a lightly floured surface, roll each ball into a 5- to 6-inch circle.

☐ Preheat oven to 450°F or highest setting. Lightly flour 2 large cookie sheets. Place 3 to 4 dough circles on each sheet and bake until just beginning to brown, about 3 minutes. Turn over and bake until lightly browned and firm to touch, 2 to 3 minutes longer. Repeat with remaining dough circles. Serve.

ABOVE BLOWING THE *SHOFAR* (RAM'S HORN) ON THE JEWISH NEW YEAR AT THE WESTERN WALL IN JERUSALEM.

KUBANEH

8 SERVINGS

This Yemenite sweet bread is eaten on the Sabbath. It is a soft, semisteamed bread which can be eaten with preserves or jams or as the Yemenites do, with a hot chutney-type relish or zhoug, a chili-paste dip. Kubaneh can be baked in the oven or on top of the stove in a very heavy-bottomed saucepan.

- 1 package active-dry yeast
- 6 tablespoons sugar
- 2 cups lukewarm water
- 4 cups all-purpose flour
- 1 teaspoon salt
- ½ teaspoon ground cinnamon or ginger
- Margarine or butter, softened, for greasing

☐ In the bowl of an electric mixer fitted with dough hook, combine yeast, 1 teaspoon sugar and ½ cup lukewarm water. Stir until yeast is almost dissolved, 1 to 2 minutes. Leave yeast mixture to stand until it looks bubbly and foamy on surface, 5 to 7 minutes.

☐ In a large bowl, combine flour, salt and cinnamon or ginger. With mixer on low speed, beat in 1½ cups lukewarm water until well blended.

☐ With machine on low speed, gradually add flour mixture and beat until mixture forms a soft dough. If mixture is very sticky, add a little more flour, but dough should be soft. Increase mixer speed to medium and knead until dough is very smooth but still soft, 5 to 7 minutes.

☐ Lightly oil a bowl. Place dough in bowl and turn to coat with oil. Cover with a clean dish towel and leave in a warm place to rise until doubled in bulk, 1½ to 2 hours.

☐ Turn out dough on to lightly floured surface and knead lightly to knock out air. Return to bowl, re-cover and leave to rise again in a warm place, about 1 hour longer.

☐ Preheat oven to 325°F. Heavily coat a 10-inch tube pan with 3 to 4 tablespoons softened margarine or butter. Turn out dough on to lightly floured surface and knead lightly to knock air out. Divide dough into 8 pieces. Roll each piece into a ball. Place balls into pan bottom just touching each other. Cover pan and leave in a warm place to rise again until balls form a ring, 30 minutes.

☐ Heavily grease a piece of foil large enough to cover pan; cover pan tightly. Bake until bread comes away from side of pan, 1¼ to 1½ hours. Carefully remove foil, lifting an edge facing away from you to allow steam to escape. If you like, continue baking, uncovered, to brown top, 15 to 20 minutes. Serve warm.

ABOVE FRESH GREEK BREAD BAKED WITH PRIDE.

OLD FASHIONED RYE BREAD

2 LOAVES

Rye bread has become associated with Jewish-deli food to such an extent that the American bread producer Levy coined the slogan "You don't have to be Jewish to eat Levy's." Rye bread is, in fact, not specifically Jewish, but the Jewish Russian and Polish bakers who went to the United States during the great wave of immigration at the end of the 19th century, baked recipes from the old country which became popular.

Rye flour is very low in gluten, so white flour is needed to lighten the texture and give the bread more body. It does make the dough more difficult to work with, so an electric mixer is helpful unless you are an expert bread maker.

- 5 cups all-purpose flour
- 3 cups rye flour
- 2 teaspoons salt
- 2 packages (2 tablespoons) active dry yeast
- 2 teaspoons sugar
- 2 tablespoons caraway seeds
- ⅓ cup vegetable oil
- 2½ cups lukewarm water
- 1 egg, beaten or 2 tablespoons butter or margarine, melted, for glaze

> ### VARIATION
>
> PREPARE DOUGH AS ABOVE BUT FORM INTO 2 OBLONG, BULLET-SHAPED LOAVES, NOT ROUNDS. AFTER GLAZING, SLASH AND SPRINKLE WITH 1 TABLESPOON ADDITIONAL CARAWAY SEEDS.

☐ In a large bowl, combine flours and salt. Set aside. In bowl of an electric mixer fitted with the dough hook, combine yeast, sugar and caraway seeds. Add oil and 1 cup lukewarm water and stir, sprinkle with a little flour. Cover bowl with a clean dish towel and leave until mixture looks slightly foamy and bubbly, 10 to 12 minutes.

☐ With mixer on low speed, pour in 1½ cups lukewarm water and beat until combined. Gradually add flours; when completely incorporated dough will be sticky. You may have some flour mixture left over.

☐ Increase mixer to medium speed and knead dough until it forms a soft ball around the dough hook and leaves side of bowl, 5 to 7 minutes. If dough remains very sticky, add a little more all-purpose flour and continue to knead 2 minutes longer. (Do not add too much more flour or bread will be tough.)

☐ Lightly grease a bowl and place dough in it; turn dough to coat with oil. (This prevents a crust from forming on surface.) Cover bowl with dish towel and leave to rise until doubled in bulk, 1½ to 2 hours, in a warm draft-free place.

☐ Lightly grease a large cookie sheet. Turn out dough on to lightly floured work surface and knead gently to knock air out of dough. Knead lightly and cut dough in half and shape each half into a smooth round ball. Place each loaf on opposite corners of cookie sheet, flatten slightly and cover with a towel. Let loaves rise until almost doubled in bulk, 1 hour.

☐ Preheat oven to 350°F. Brush loaves with egg glaze or melted butter or margarine. With a sharp knife, slash top of each loaf 2 or 3 times. Bake until loaves are well browned and sound hollow when tapped on bottom, 35 to 40 minutes. Remove to a wire rack to cool. (This prevents bottom from becoming soggy.)

ABOVE FRESH BAGUETTES IN A COUNTRY BAKERY IN NORMANDY, FRANCE.

CHALLAH

2 LOAVES

Challah is the traditional, braided egg bread served on the Sabbath and other Jewish holidays. It is usually braided, except at Rosh Hashana when a special spiral loaf is prepared to symbolize reaching for heaven in the hope of a happy New Year. This is the most popular egg bread in the United States and one of the most versatile because its soft, yellow, cake-like crumb suits most foods very well.

- 1 package active-dry yeast
- 1 tablespoon sugar
- ⅓ cup lukewarm water
- 1 teaspoon salt
- 5 tablespoons vegetable oil
- 2 eggs, lightly beaten
- 6 cups all-purpose flour, sifted
- 1 egg, beaten with a pinch of salt and pinch of sugar, for glazing
- Sesame or poppy seeds

VARIATION

TO FORM THE TRADITIONAL ROSH HASHANA SPIRAL LOAF, PREPARE DOUGH AS ABOVE BUT ROLL EACH DOUGH HALF INTO 1 LONG SAUSAGE SHAPE ABOUT 24 INCHES LONG AND 1 INCH IN DIAMETER. HOLD ONE END AGAINST THE SURFACE AND USING IT AS THE CENTER, BEGIN COILING THE SPIRAL AROUND ON ITSELF SO DOUGH FORMS CONCENTRIC CIRCLES. PLACE ON UPPER LEFT-HAND CORNER OF COOKIE SHEET AND TUCK ONE END UNDER LOAF. REPEAT WITH SECOND PIECE OF DOUGH, PLACING IT DIAGONALLY OPPOSITE IT IN THE LOWER RIGHT-HAND CORNER OF COOKIE SHEET AND BAKE AS FOR BRAIDED LOAVES.

☐ In the bowl of an electric mixer with dough hook fitted, combine yeast and sugar. Stir in water. Sprinkle with a little flour to cover. Cover with a clean dish towel and leave until mixture looks slightly foamy and bubbly, 10 to 12 minutes.

☐ With mixer on low speed, beat in salt, oil and eggs until well mixed. Gradually add flour; when completely incorporated dough will be slightly sticky. Increase mixer to medium speed and knead dough until dough forms a ball around the dough hook and leaves side of bowl, 5 to 7 minutes. If dough remains sticky, add a little more flour and continue to knead 2 minutes longer. (Do not add too much flour; a softer dough yields a moister loaf.)

☐ Lightly grease a large bowl. Place dough in it, turn dough to coat with oil. (This prevents a crust from forming on the surface.) Cover with a clean dish towel and leave to rise until doubled in bulk, 1½ to 2 hours, in a moderately warm, draft-free place; do not leave to rise in too warm a place or texture may be uneven.

☐ Turn out dough on to lightly floured work surface and knead gently. Return dough to bowl, cover tightly and refrigerate 6 to 8 hours or overnight to let dough rise slowly a second time. (Allowing dough to rise slowly provides a light, even texture.)

☐ Turn out dough on to a lightly floured work surface and knead gently. Shape into a ball and cut into 2 equal-size pieces.

☐ Lightly grease a large cookie sheet. Working with one half at a time, cut dough half into 3 equal-size pieces; roll into balls. Roll each ball into long sausage shapes about 18 inches long and 1 inch wide. Braid the 3 sausage shapes together and place on one side of cookie sheet, tucking ends neatly underneath loaf. Repeat with remaining dough to form second loaf.

☐ Cover loaves with clean dish towel and leave in a warm place to rise until almost doubled in size, 1 hour. Preheat oven to 375°F.

☐ Brush each risen loaf with egg glaze and sprinkle with sesame or poppy seeds. Bake 40 minutes until loaves are well browned and sound hollow when tapped on the bottom. Remove to a wire rack to cool.